D1524793

Success in Kindergarten Reading and Writing

The Readiness Concept of the Future

ADDITIONAL TITLES IN THE SUCCESS IN READING AND WRITING SERIES

Success in Beginning Reading and Writing
Anne H. Adams

Phonics/Spelling Activity Sheets for use with Success in Beginning Reading and Writing

Success in Reading and Writing, Grade Two
Anne H. Adams and Helen Cappleman

Success in Reading and Writing, Grade Three
Anne H. Adams and Mary S. Johnson

Success in Reading and Writing, Grade Four
Anne H. Adams, Jean Bernholz, Pat Sumner

Success in Reading and Writing, Grade Five
Anne H. Adams, Jean Bernholz, Pat Sumner

Success in Reading and Writing, Grade Six
Anne H. Adams and Elizabeth Bebensee

Success in Kindergarten Reading and Writing

The Readiness Concept of the Future

Anne H. Adams
Mary S. Johnson
Judith M. Connors

Good Year Books • Glenview, Illinois

Library of Congress Cataloging in Publication Data

ADAMS, ANNE H
Success in kindergarten reading and writing.

(Success in reading and writing series)
Bibliography:
Includes index.

1. Language arts (Preschool) 2. Kindergarten—Methods and manuals. 3. Reading readiness. I. Johnson, Mary S., joint author. II. Connors, Judith M., joint author. III. Title. IV. Series.

LB1181.A3 372.6 80-14556

ISBN: 0-673-16437-3

78910-HAD-898887

ISBN: 0-673-16437-3

Contents

Preface

The kindergartner lives in a world of print and flashing words. *Sesame Street*, *The Electric Company*, and Saturday morning cartoons are just three of the constant factors in the lives of the majority of pre-first graders. As these children sit for hours immersed in television, a large number of words and phrases shown on the screen become a part of their early education. In an automobile, they learn to read *Texaco*, *McDonalds*, *STOP*, etc., with no difficulty whatsoever. At breakfast they point to words on a favorite cereal box and want to know what they mean. The day of the nonreader in kindergarten will soon pass, if it is not already gone.

Almost without exception, young children *want* to learn to read and write. They equate these skills wih a natural part of their inheritance and approach them as a form of play. They are eager and ready to read and write. The kindergarten and/or the home is the place to encourage the desire of young children who want to learn, not to turn off that desire or delay it.

There is nothing magical concerning chronological age five with reference to reading and writing. Unfortunately, some people feel a child should be six years old before he or she can receive reading/writing instruction. Strangely, among these same people are those who bemoan the fact that there are so many older students experiencing difficulty in reading and writing. Early confidence in reading and writing is a must if children are to avoid experiencing feelings of academic failure.

Whether reading should or should not be taught in kindergarten is a controversial matter. The authors of the *Success in Kindergarten Reading and Writing* program do not take sides on the issue. Our position is that kindergarten should provide a program that will afford opportunities for children to learn to read/write *if they can and if they wish to do so.* For children who do not learn to read/write prior to or during kindergarten, the program should encompass cognate components that are as enjoyable as the reading/writing ones. This is capsuled in the *Success* program.

Children can and should be exposed to reading and writing instruction in the kindergarten; however, there are positive and negative ways of providing the introduction. *Success in Kindergarten Reading and Writing* endorses the concept of incorporating instruction with the developmental process of each child, instead of predetermining a developmental sequence and then trying to make each child fit into it. Brzeinski and Howard support this concept.

> Today, the desirability of early childhood education in reading is well documented.

> Researchers suggest that we must reorder our educational priorities; we must give additional emphasis to early childhood education.[1]

They assert that there is a "wealth of research data that supports the success and potential of early childhood reading."[2]

The *Success* program incorporates (1) the child's vocabulary, (2) printed words from familiar items in the child's environment, and (3) a flexible structure that enables the teacher to develop program content that varies each day based on student input. Students improve their reading/writing abilities almost as naturally as they once learned to speak and listen.

The *Success* program does *not* endorse either of two extremes: (1) the "let-them-play-all-day" camp; or (2) the "make-them-learn" camp. It does credit the intelligence of today's kindergarten children, their teachers and parents, and endorses the concept that we have children who watch complicated television plots, endlessly ask "why" questions, and are completely open to wanting more information, more skills, and more education. As this enthusiasm is incorporated into the basic kindergarten program, we begin a generation of children who enter first grade already feeling comfortable and successful with the reading and writing process, and wanting more of the same feelings and experiences. The modules of the *Success* program are designed to facilitate the incorporation of reading and writing into each kindergartner's world as naturally as he or she plays, speaks, or listens.

The *Success in Beginning Reading and Writing*[3] program was introduced in 1976–77 in first grade classes in Durham (North Carolina) City Schools. At the end of that year, these inner city students, according to statistics released by the Durham City Schools, averaged at the 74th percentile on the Comprehensive Tests of Basic Skills, 24 points *above* the national average, rather than at the 23rd percentile, where previous students had averaged in this system. The positive *had* taken place, and students who weren't supposed to be able to read and write independently were doing just that.

During the piloting of the *Success* program in the first grades, some parents and kindergarten teachers expressed a need for the concepts of the first level *Success* program to be initiated in the kindergarten. A major component requested was a program that would introduce pre-first graders to a variety of reading and writing activities through a structure that mandates flexibility of both content and instruction. There was no objection to children learning to read and write in the kindergarten; however, if some did not learn, at least they would not enter first grade without ever being exposed to the techniques of reading and writing.

Due to requests from parents for a program that could be used independently in the home or in open correlation and reinforcement with the school's kindergarten program, the concepts and activities presented in the *Success in Kindergarten Reading and Writing* program have been adapted for parents to use at home with their young children. Emphasis is placed on an informal, relaxed atmosphere in the home that provides opportunities for the pre-first grade child to experience success with the reading/writing process.

The first pilot classes of the *Success* kindergarten program began in September, 1977. During that year, the authors made modifications in the lessons based on teacher recommendations which, in part, came from the student responses in the classrooms. Content and methodologies of the pilot lessons had been researched and prepared over a ten-year period prior to their piloting.

Perhaps the *Success* concept can be summarized in the words of Mr. John Howard, principal of Pearson School in the Durham City Schools, who after visiting one of the *Success* kindergarten classes told one of the authors, "I was just in a kindergarten class, and those children are reading and writing. They don't seem to think there's anything unusual about it."

[1]Joseph E. Brzeinski and Will Howard, "Early Reading—How, Not When!" *The Reading Teacher* 25:241, 1971.

[2]*Ibid.*, p. 239.

[3]Goodyear Publishing Company, 1978.

Acknowledgments

The authors wish to express appreciation to Vanessa Brice and her kindergarten students at Pearson School in the Durham (North Carolina) City Schools for some of the student's work included in this book; to Patsy Suggs, kindergarten teacher, for program logistics suggestions;

To Mary Jane McReynolds, Assistant Superintendent for Instruction, Wake County Schools, for encouraging the development of the *Success* kindergarten program;

To Ben T. Brooks, Superintendent of the Durham City Schools, who demonstrated administrative leadership in improving education;

To John Howard, principal of Pearson School, who supports the concept of improving kindergarten programs;

To Margaret Munford, principal of Watts Street School in Durham;

To Joyce Wasdell, Assistant Superintendent for Instruction in the Durham County Schools;

To Alma Stokes, John Taylor, and Dorothy Melvin, principals in the Greensboro (North Carolina) Schools; Ed Lane, Earl Watson, George Cooper, Ed Comer, and Joanne Cooper, principals in the Wake County Schools, and to Charles Sigmon, principal of Winterfield School in the Charlott-Mecklenburg (North Carolina) Schools for their belief in the capabilities of kindergarten students;

To Mary Frances Peete, Assistant Director of the Duke University Reading Center;

To the following teachers: Jane Allen, Linda Batten, Merilyn Beezer, Pam Bridges, Alenna Brooks, Frances Dean, Peggy Dunfee, Marilyn Gehner, Sherry Mall, Jeanne Heidenreich, Fern Hines, Helen Holz, Patricia Hooper, Kristen Louise Kain, Kathy Kulla, Lelia F. Lindsay, Betty Mullins, Martha Proffitt, Ann Rhyne, Ashlyn Ross, Maureen Sorrenson, Carolyn Simms, Jan Taylor, Sandra T. Walker, and Jean Whitmire for the work they have accomplished in teaching students;

To Janet Snyder, Elementary Reading Program Development Specialist, Jefferson County (Kentucky) Public Schools;

To Carol Johnson, Director of Elementary Curriculum Development, Bloomfield Hills (Michigan) School District;

To Jasper Harvey, Bureau of Education for the Handicapped, United States Office of Education, and to James Jenkins, Director of the Division of Early Childhood Education, North Carolina State Department of Public Instruction for their pioneer work in kindergarten education;

To Ina Tabibian, Goodyear Publishing Company;

To Charles M. Campbell, educator and legislator, and Kenneth Yamamoto, Director of Reading for the State of Hawaii;

To Anne Flowers, Professor and Chairman of the Duke University Department of Education;

To Ruth Chadwick, principal of the Horace Mann School in Newton, Massachusetts;

To Lenore Parker, Professor, Lesley College, Cambridge, Massachusetts;

To Gale Lambright, Professor, University of South Alabama;

To the memory of Jerry Keen, an educator who believed in quality education and the expertise of teachers;

To Otto Fridai, Assistant Superintendent for Instruction, Dallas (Texas) Independent Schools;

To Alfred Roberts, principal of the Paul L. Dunbar Community Learning Center, Dallas City Schools;

To Helen M. Adams, for reading the manuscript;

To the hundreds of preschool teachers with whom the authors have had the opportunity to confer and work, and to the many parents whose concern prompted us to research and pilot the *Success in Kindergarten Reading and Writing* program and write this book;

And especially to Caroline Massengill and her students at Swift Creek School in the Wake County (North Carolina) Public School System.

chapter one

Getting Ready to Teach the Success Program

THE BASIC ASSUMPTION

The Success in Kindergarten Reading and Writing *program is based on the assumption that reading and writing are integral parts of a kindergarten student's life and are not separate entities apart from or foreign to the child.*

OBJECTIVES

By the end of the kindergarten year, each student will have had many opportunities to

1. *Observe* the writing of selected words spoken by each student.
2. *Say* the name of each letter as it is written by someone.
3. *Write* words selected by that student.
4. *Associate* words with tangible items and intangible concepts in pictures.
5. *Read* words printed in a variety of materials.
6. *Absorb* the reading/writing process in natural rather than artificial ways.
7. *Transcend* the barrier from illiteracy to the beginnings of literacy.
8. *Be proud* of academic accomplishments as one aspect of a positive self-concept.
9. *Learn* to interact with other children while involved in reading/writing experiences.
10. *Improve* listening and speaking abilities with a wide variety and large number of printed and written words.
11. *Participate* in the above objectives to the extent of individual abilities and interests.

Each of the above objectives should be realized to some degree every day by each student in kindergarten. The *Success* lessons are designed to assist you in helping each student achieve the objectives.

OVERVIEW OF LESSON COMPONENTS

The *Success* lessons are found in Appendix One, and there is one lesson for each of 180 school days. A lesson consists of three modules scheduled for approximately twenty minutes each: Picture/Word Association

Module, Alphabet Module, Story Time Module, and the Oral Language/Reading Module, taught on an individual teacher-to-student basis at a convenient time during each day.

Each module emphasizes a different approach to introduce children to the knowledge of written letter symbol combinations and comprehension of written words, phrases, and sentences. Because the approaches differ, provision is made in the program for balance, reinforcement, and variety of instruction. In addition, internal emphases within each module change to incorporate new dimensions as the kindergarten year progresses.

Here is how the modules differ, achieving the balance and variety of components within the *Success* program:

The *Picture/Word Association Modules* emphasize the concept of reading words for tangible items, such as *air conditioner vent, ears, brown,* and intangibles such as *love* and *sharing* associated with pictures, instead of simply "reading pictures" without an organized approach.

The *Alphabet Modules,* most of which are correlated with art, emphasize the concept of writing a sequence of letters to form words. The words are volunteered from members of the class rather than from a predetermined published list.

The *Oral Language/Reading Modules* emphasize the concept of an individual child watching his or her words being written and used in oral expressions by another person. These modules are taught on an individual teacher-to-student basis at any convenient time during the school day.

The *Story Time Modules* emphasize the concept of listening to an adult read stories while stressing categories of words that the students hear in the stories.

The four modules in the *Success* program incorporate traditional reading/writing readiness components, such as the use of pictures, art, puppets, stories, and the students' own self-expressions. In addition, the modules provide a base plan that correlates these components and affords the expansion of their dimensions.

FIGURE 1-1 Example Of One Lesson

LESSON	PICTURE/WORD ASSOCIATION MODULE	ALPHABET MODULE	ORAL LANGUAGE/ READING MODULE	STORY TIME MODULE
1	(Part I of lesson)	(Part II of lesson)	(Part III of lesson)	(Part IV of lesson)
	Teacher records on chart paper words suggested by students concerning **people** in a magazine picture. Chart is displayed in the class for several days. It is then put on a chart stand.	Students practice writing the letter **1** on paper and do an art drawing. Paper is dated and filed in a manila folder in a box labeled **Alphabet Module Papers.**	At a convenient time during the day, the teacher records at least one word spoken by a student about the theme **toys.** The teacher writes the word on a strip of construction paper and the student displays the strip in the classroom. This procedure is repeated with another student.	Teacher writes names of some of the **characters** on the chalkboard or on chart paper prior to reading the story. Teacher occasionally points to the names on the board as they appear in the story.
	Module taught for approximately 20 minutes.	Module taught for approximately 20 minutes.	(No block of time—teacher touches base with individual students anytime.)	(Module taught for approximately 20 minutes)

Figure 1–1 is an example of one lesson.

Teacher expertise is highly valued in this program. In fact, no two teachers will teach any module exactly alike. Teachers should develop the module in a teaching style comfortable to them and enjoyable to the students. It is important, however, that the base format of each module be followed.

Although each lesson in Appendix One contains suggested instructional emphases, you may wish to substitute other talking, listening, reading, or writing emphases. Flexibility is one of the strong features of the *Success* program. For example, one teacher may use an entirely different picture in the first module in Lesson 5 from the picture used by another teacher. One teacher may insert a song related to the theme of the third module in Lesson 32 while another teacher may use a different activity to expand the module.

The *Success* program recognizes the fact that each teacher has the intelligence and expertise to make unique contributions to improving the instructional program. The base structure of the *Success* modules are intended to make it easier for teachers to incorporate activities into an educationally sound framework that includes an introduction to reading and writing.

SCHEDULING MODULES WITHIN A LESSON

You should schedule three 20-minute teaching times when the majority of the children are in the classroom. The 20 minutes for the first, second, and fourth modules are suggested time guidelines only and are *not* rigid requirements. Some days a module will take less than 20 minutes; some days a module will take longer. The important point is not to omit a module, or extend one at the expense of another. Figure 1–2 is an example of a schedule for *Success* modules. A schedule such as this should be *posted outside the classroom door*. This is one way to help students develop a sense of time, and the idea of scheduling selected internal school components.

Begin the program by teaching Lesson 1. The next day, teach Lesson 2. Although references to themes, letters, and words in previous lessons can be made as a form of review or reinforcement, do not *emphasize* the same topic or letter for two consecutive days. The *Success* program includes a wealth of topics and activities instead of narrow or limited dimensions.

This program is not intended to take a full day. Construction activities, music, center times, and other traditional components of the kindergarten program should continue. Teachers of this program who had students for a full day had no difficulty scheduling the four modules and the other activities each day. If the students are in school for only a half-day, the amount of time for each module should be reduced by half. The half-day schedule would necessitate fewer students participating in each module; therefore, you must make sure that all students, over a period of a few days, have opportunities to participate in each module.

MATERIALS

It is possible, though not ideal, to teach the *Success* program without the purchase of the following consumable materials, provided teachers are willing to bring magazines, newspapers, and comics to class. If the budget permits, however, these materials should be provided for each kindergarten class:

1. Three subscriptions to a local newspaper per day, Monday–Friday per class. (Some students may enter school able to read the newspaper; others recognize specialized words, names of people, or trade names.)

FIGURE 1–2 Sample Schedule For Modules

9:00 - 9:20 —	PICTURE/WORD ASSOCIATION MODULE
10:10 - 10:30 —	ALPHABET MODULE
With individuals at various times during the day —	ORAL LANGUAGE/READING MODULE
1:30 - 1:50 —	STORY TIME MODULE

2. Subscriptions to five magazines such as *Sesame Street, Jack and Jill, National Geographic, Humpty Dumpty, Wee Wisdom, Ebony, Progressive Farmer, Sports Illustrated, Electric Company, Wildlife.*
3. Subscriptions to five comic books such as *Donald Duck, Batman, Super Heroes, Tarzan, The Incredible Hulk, Chip and Dale, Daffy Duck.*
4. One copy of *Success in Kindergarten Reading and Writing* for the teacher.
5. One dictionary for the teacher.
6. Ten to fifteen student dictionaries.
7. 180 sheets of large size unlined chart paper, such as newsprint.
8. Construction paper, scissors, paste, crayons, Magic Markers, masking tape.
9. Unlined writing paper for students.
10. Small paper bags, socks, etc., for making puppets.
11. Catalogues such as *Sears, Montgomery Ward.*
12. Forty to fifty library books rotated every two weeks.
13. Boxes such as cereal boxes, toy boxes, model airplane boxes.

NEWSPAPERS IN THE KINDERGARTEN

Each day during the year you should refer to some part of the newspaper by holding it up before the class, pointing to an article, advertisement, or comic frame and discussing the contents. It is best if a current newspaper is used. Since parents may discuss current events at home, and television reports cover many of the same topics, inclusion of information from newspapers in the kindergarten increases opportunities for parent/child communication at home. Some kindergarten teachers have the "Newspaper Reports" at the beginning of the Story Time Module; others schedule it as an opening activity each morning; others have it during the day but at no set time; others, unfortunately, do not include the newspaper in the kindergarten program at all.

Every fifth lesson in the Alphabet Module beginning with Lesson 1 and continuing through Lesson 72 includes the use of newspapers and/or magazines. Students tear or cut out sections from the newspaper, paste them on paper, and circle or underline a specific letter(s).

There are many other activities that students can do using newspapers; however, at the kindergarten level, the emphasis should be on introducing them to the concept of the newspaper as a daily vehicle containing many kinds of information.

MAGAZINES IN THE KINDERGARTEN

Magazines have an enormous variety of pictures and words in different sizes of print. For kindergarten, the major value of the magazine is the pictures. Use large magazine pictures extensively in the first module, Picture/Word Association Module. Use any size magazine pictures in the third module, Oral Language/Reading Module, beginning with Lesson 81. In the first module, each student points to one item in the picture and responds to the item. Later in the year, in the third module, each student cuts or tears out a picture or part of a picture and watches you record his or her words on the picture (or written by the student if he or she can write). Kindergarten students also like to browse through magazines.

COMICS IN THE KINDERGARTEN

There are no distinct modules for using comics within any lesson in the *Success* program; however, the vast majority of kindergarten children love to "get lost" in comic books. By having them in the classroom, students will gravitate on an irregular basis to comic books—at times even during some of the free center time.

DICTIONARIES IN THE KINDERGARTEN

The Alphabet Module, beginning with Lesson 53, is where kindergartners especially like to locate words beginning with a certain letter or letter combination, using the dictionary as one tool to find the words. The object is to introduce students to dictionaries, not to emphasize reading words in the dictionary. Most kindergartners take delight in finding a word with a certain letter cluster and asking what it means. Others who do not want to use a dictionary do not have to do so.

LIBRARY BOOKS IN THE KINDERGARTEN

Unfortunately, even today some schools may not permit first graders to go to the school library, much less kindergarten students. Some children come from homes where parents read books or take them to the public library and thus they probably have had more exposure to books. However, not all pre-first graders have had this exposure.

At least 40 library books should be *in the kindergarten classroom* and rotated back into the library every two weeks in exchange for 40 different books so each student will have the chance to handle these kinds of printed materials in his or her own way. Favorite books should remain in the kindergarten classroom for longer than two weeks. In addition, the *Success* program recommends that you read at least one book or part of a book to the students each day during the Story Time Module.

chapter two

How to Teach the Picture/Word Association Module

The Picture/Word Association Module is found in the second column of each lesson in Appendix One. The major purposes of this module are to provide opportunities each day for students to (1) volunteer *their* words associated with a variety of pictures, (2) observe the formation of each letter within the words as it is written, and (3) possibly, read the words individually or with the group.

The fact that *students* rather than adults volunteer the words used in this module is extremely important. Kindergartners in rural Wyoming will volunteer locally used words that are different from those volunteered in Atlanta, Georgia. On the other hand, there is a vast common bank of words used by both groups. This module accommodates both kinds of words.

HOW TO TEACH THE PICTURE/WORD ASSOCIATION MODULE

This is the first module of a lesson and should last for an average of 20 minutes. According to kindergarten teachers, the time for this module ranges from 10 to 30 minutes, depending almost exclusively on the amount of discussion about topics identified within the module.

As the year progresses, students improve their ability to listen, (which is one of the inherent parts of this module), to locate items in the pictures with greater speed, and to work with other students as they learn to wait their turn, listen to others, and associate oral language with written words. During the first *days* of the school year, the key is to make sure that *each* student participates in some way—volunteering words, spelling, discussing a description, drawing a line on the chart paper, adding to a response made by another child—within the Picture/Word Association Modules. You should not overcall on those students who usually have the "right answer" or a "ready answer" at the expense of neglecting other students.

There are three major parts within each Picture/Word Association Module: (1) the readiness part, (2), the student vocabulary part, and (3) the display part.

The Readiness Part—Each Day

1. Look at the Picture/Word Association Module column in Appendix One and note the theme. Select a picture (see the section on pictorial aids in Chapter One) or draw one that *can be associated* with the theme. For example, if the theme is *automobile tires*, the picture could be a full-page magazine advertisement about a particular car for sale. In the picture there would be tires on the car. The picture should have *much*

detail in it. Do not use a picture depicting *only* tires. Early in the year, you select the pictures yourself; later, students can look through magazines to locate pictures appropriate to a Picture/Word Association Module's theme and put one or more pictures on chart paper.

2. Tape a large sheet of unlined chart paper, such as newsprint, on the chalkboard.

3. Tape the picture in the center of the chart paper.

4. Ask the students to sit in a semicircle or informally in a group on the floor as near as possible to the picture on the chart paper.

5. As each of the above four steps are being accomplished, the teacher ad-libs about the picture, asking individual students appropriate questions about some aspects in the picture or its general theme.

The Readiness Phase sets the scene for direct input from the students, and establishes thematic directions for that input.

The Student Vocabulary Part—Each Day

As soon as the picture has been put up and a short discussion (no longer than two minutes) has established the theme, begin the Student Vocabulary Part of the Picture/Word Association Module.

6. Ask the group to think of a title for the picture either *before* or *after* the items in the picture are named. Use your expertise to guide the discussion and condense it into a title. As the year progresses, students learn how to create titles.

7. Write the title at the top of the chart, calling attention to the fact that important words in the title begin with a capital letter. *Say each letter as you write it,* and ask the students to say it either with you or as they hear you pronounce it. Do not wait to say the letters after the word is written. *Do not emphasize the sound of any letter in this module.*

One objective of this module is to afford student opportunities to observe the writing of as many different letters as possible according to their placement within words. As the words are written on the chart paper, the object is *not* to isolate any of the thousands of sound combinations within words or to dwell on the particular sound of one or two particular letters. An introduction to certain letter sounds is included in some phases in the Alphabet Module. The only time letter sounds are used in the Picture/Word Association Module is later in the year when a student, instead of the teacher, is writing on the chart paper and the class and teacher are helping determine which letter to write next. The decoding aspects learned in the Alphabet Module then become useful in the Picture/Word Association Module.

8. Ask one student in the group to come up to the picture, point to one item, and say its name. As the student stands at the chalkboard, use a Magic Marker to write the word(s) volunteered by the student, *voicing the name of each letter as it is written* and then saying the letters with the rest of the students as they hear them.

9. The student who volunteered the word(s) then uses a Magic Marker to draw a line from the item in the picture to the word(s) written by the teacher.

10. Another student comes up to the chart, points to a different item in the picture, and says the name of the item. Write the word while orally spelling each letter, while the student draws a line from his or her item identified in the picture to the word you write.

11. After Lesson 20 is completed, help students develop a sentence that contains *some* of the words written on the chart. Write the sentence at the bottom of the chart, spelling each letter with the students as you write it. Comment about capitalization at the beginning of the sentence and/or proper nouns, compound words, and punctuation marks. The class then "reads" the sentence orally while you point to each word in the sentence.

Throughout the Student Vocabulary Part of this module, there should be a dialogue between teacher and students about the topics and words. You should write as fast as possible and retain legibility so as many students as possible have the opportunity to come up to the chart.

It is during this informal format that you have opportunities to insert many kinds of information other than meaning of words and situations in which words are found. You should informally comment on matters such as capitalization, plurals, compound words, and contractions. As the year progresses, many students absorb this information and begin to use it in their own writing.

Subject areas or units can be incorporated easily in the Picture/Word Association Module. For example, if a student points to an eye and says *eye*, you might ask, "How many eyes do you see in the picture?" If the student replies *two eyes*, write *two eyes* on the chart paper and emphasize that the *s* at the end of the word *eye* means more than one eye. This correlates with mathematics and plurals in an informal, enjoyable manner.

Do not insist that every student volunteer a word each day. Shy or reluctant students, especially at the beginning of the year, should be asked if they would like to find something in the picture; however, if the response is "No," you should say "Perhaps you'll like to find something tomorrow." When these students learn there is no threat involved, they will want to give it a try. As soon as possible, each student in the class should have the opportunity to participate in the module *each day*.

You should write the words at the beginning of the year. When a student learns to write, and wants to write—even one letter in a word—you should ask that student to come up to the chart and write the letter while you and the class say it. Eventually, other students in the class will want to write words on the class chart paper. Do not discourage this, and do not expect their letters to be "beautifully" formed. Each day during the year, the abilities of the students increase.

During the last two months of 1978–79, visitors to a pilot *Success* class were amazed at the following scene:

> A kindergarten child uncapped the Magic Marker, stood before the group, and asked another child to come to the chart. After the child had pointed to the picture and said the word *brown*, the class spelled the word without hesitation while one of their peers wrote the word *brown*, and a line was drawn from the word to a brown-colored part in the picture. Then a second student came to the chart, pointed to the picture, and said *air conditioner vent*. The young writer started writing the words, while members of the class orally spelled each letter. Another student replaced the writer at the chart and the procedure was repeated until each child had his or her turn.
>
> The teacher was sitting on the floor with the students and the only time her voice was heard was when a rough spot was encountered in an irregular spelling within a word volunteered by one of the students. To the students, it was a game—a form of play—to unlock these words and watch them appear on the chart paper. To the visitors, it was an eye-opener.

The Display Part — Ten-Day Cycles

When each student has had an opportunity to contribute input to the picture on the chart paper, you should remove the chart from the chalkboard and display it in some part of the classroom where it can be seen by all students. Display each chart for ten days before taking down the first chart on the eleventh day and putting it on a chart stand. Replace the first chart with the eleventh chart. On the twelfth day, replace the second chart with the twelfth-day chart and put the second chart on a chart stand.

It is extremely important that the students' words and *their* chart be visible in the classroom—on the bulletin boards, beside windows, on the front of the teacher's desk, above the chalkboard, etc. The students not only are very proud of their charts, but they like to return to them on their own time and associate words they know on the charts with the pictures.

Note the example of a chart, in Figure 2–1, developed by a kindergarten class during Lesson 1. In this particular classroom, the teacher drew a face and the students volunteered various parts of the body that should be added. The teacher drew and labeled the parts according to words suggested by the students. No attempt was made by the teacher in this first module to have a "perfect drawing." In another classroom, a different teacher teaching this same lesson, used a picture of a face in a magazine advertisement. In both classrooms, the words on the charts were volunteered by individual students in the class.

Figure 2–2 is an example of a chart developed in a kindergarten class during the Picture/Word Association Module in Lesson 6 (the sixth day of the program). Note that the module theme for Lesson 6 is *furniture*, and the students volunteered single words. The teacher selected a picture that had some furniture in it, and the students decided to title this particular picture, "Pretty Room."

Figure 2–3 is an example of a chart developed later in the year in Lesson 46 (46th day of the program). More students have volunteered words, and

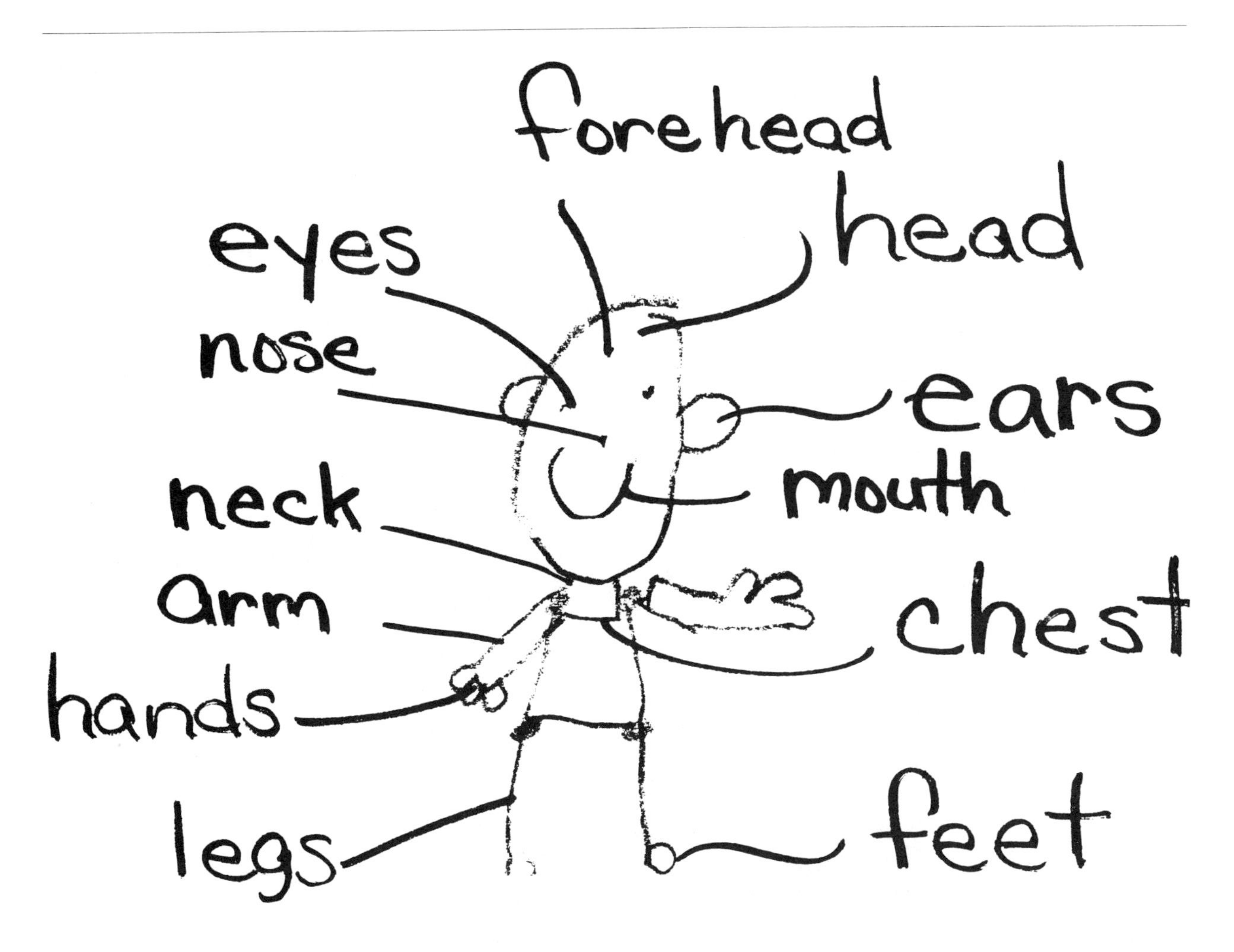

FIGURE 2-1 **Example of A Chart Developed in Lesson 1, Picture Word Association Module**

there is a greater variety of words. Note also the word clusters on the chart: *crunchy cereal, big ears, white napkin, table top, a fat cat.* The theme suggestion for Lesson 46 is *eyes.* The teacher of this class selected a picture of a cat. While taping the picture on the chart paper, the teacher talked about the cat's eyes, what eyes do, different colors of eyes, and emphasized the concept of eyes only during that Readiness Part of the module. This particular picture was in color, hence the "color words" on the chart. Once the students come to the chart, they should not be restricted to talk only about the topic of eyes, but encouraged to refer to any item in the picture.

THE PHASES WITHIN THE ACADEMIC YEAR

There are three Phases in the Picture/Word Association Module extending throughout the academic year. During Phase I, at the beginning of the year, students may not be able to accomplish the same kinds of activities they perform with ease during Phase III near the end of the year. For example, a student during the first days of school may not wish to volunteer a word for an item he or she sees in a picture. As the year progresses, with daily exposure, no pressure, and observation of the enjoyment of other students who are doing this, the same students may overcome shyness or lack of ability and enter

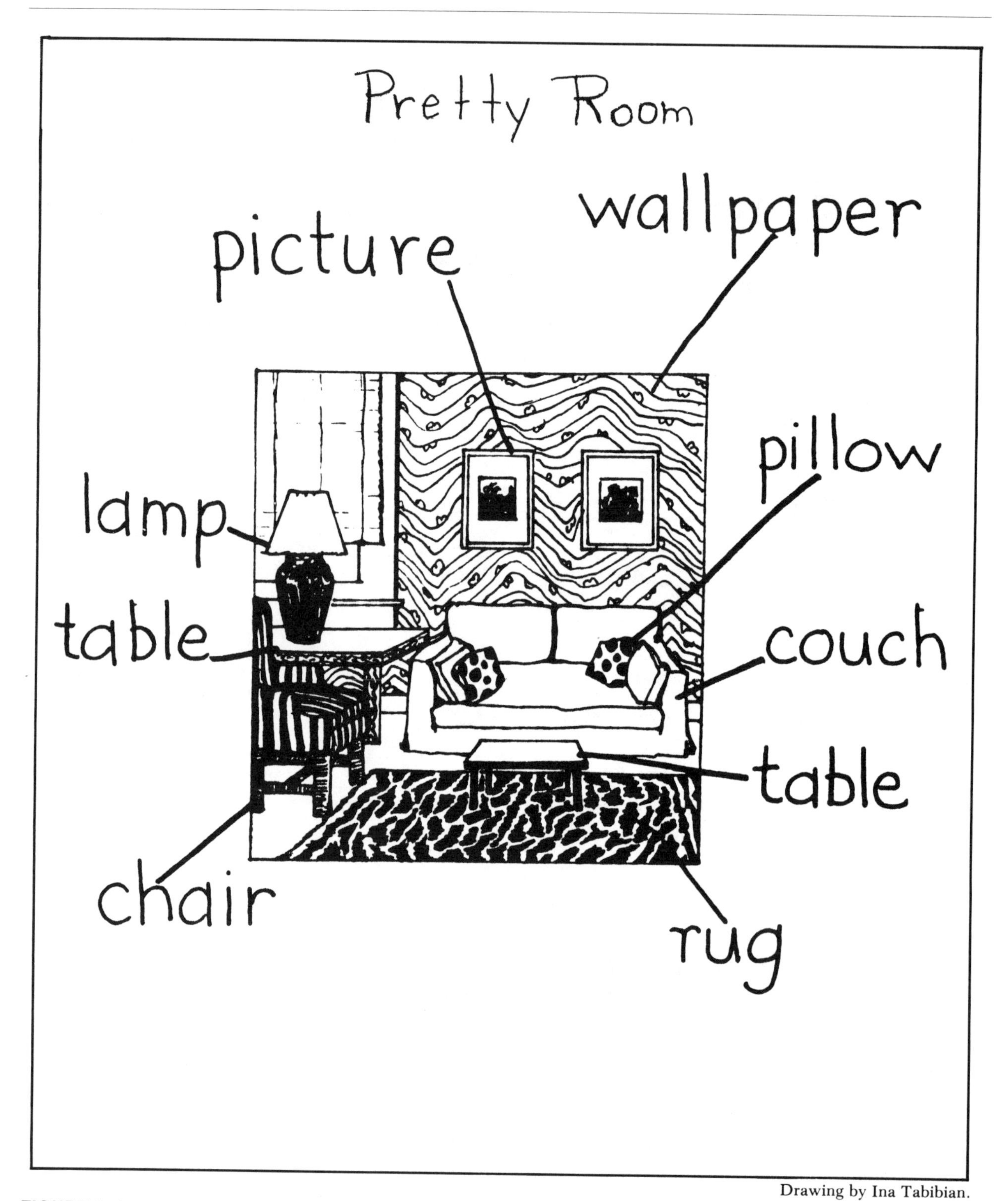

Drawing by Ina Tabibian.

FIGURE 2-2 **Example of a Chart from Lesson 6, Picture/Word Association Module**

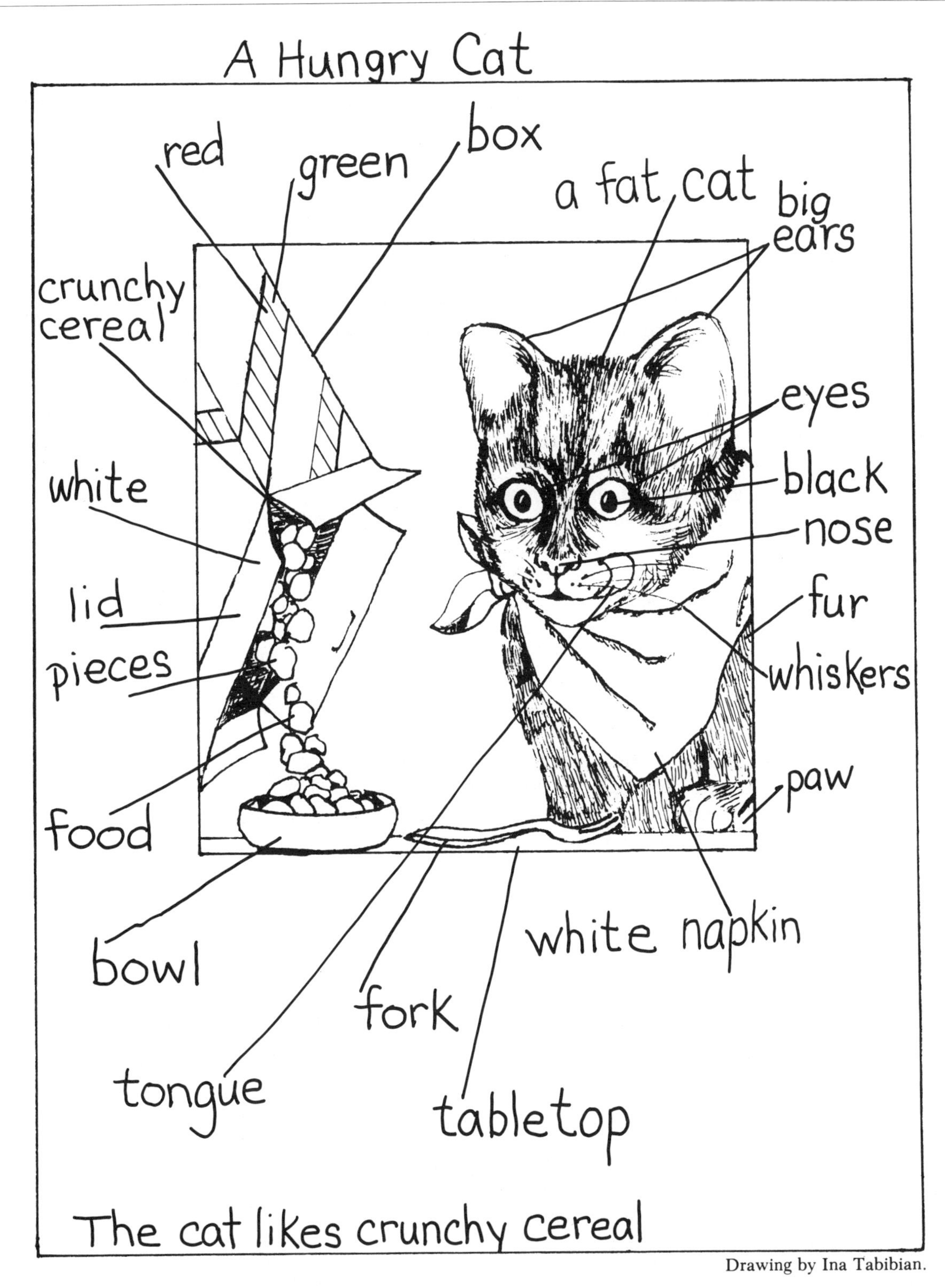

Drawing by Ina Tabibian.

FIGURE 2-3 **Example of a Chart from Lesson 46, Picture/Word Association Module**

the activity willingly and with pleasure. The point is not to give up on students or exclude them from the possibility of being a part of the activity because they cannot complete the task at one instance in their educational experience. With positive encouragement and enough opportunities, they can become participants in many ways. For some the ability comes later in the year than for others, just as some toddlers walk with greater accuracy sooner than other toddlers—yet almost all of them eventually learn to walk with confidence.

Now we will see how one Phase leads into the next Phase, which has a different focus, yet incorporates the emphasis of the preceding Phase(s).

Phase I incorporates the first 40 lessons of the Picture/Word Association Module, where the emphasis is on the teacher writing *single words* for items identified by students. The emphasis does not prevent you from writing more than one word volunteered by a student, or even from writing a sentence; however, the majority of the words written during Phase I should be single words. Figure 2-2 is an example of a chart from Lesson 6, from Phase I. In addition during this Phase, students are learning the format and process of how this module is conducted. Most important of all, the students are introduced to the reading/writing process of *their words* and the words of their classmates. At the beginning of the year, the association may be remote. As the year progresses, students will become more proficient in locating and verbalizing associations. You should assist students who want to try but are not sure how to go about it. Ask leading questions such as, "What color is the box?" and write the child's response *"blue"*; or "Where is the box?" and write *chair* from the child's response *on the chair."*

For the first 20 days of Phase I, a part of the instructional format includes students learning that they will have opportunities to talk and listen to others talk about the picture. During these first days, some take longer than others to learn to become a part of the group and there may be fewer words on the chart than will be volunteered later in the year. You should try to involve each student several times by asking questions. The discussion should move briskly, getting as many words as possible on the chart. Early in the year, some students who are reluctant to volunteer a word may come to the chart and trace a line. All students can do something. Relax, and enjoy teaching the module.

On the 20th day, the first step in sentence composing is undertaken. Do not be discouraged if you experience difficulty or if the sentence does not develop immediately in class. Each day thereafter, attempts to form sentences as the last part of the Picture/Word Association Module should be made. Each day there are opportunities for learning.

The emphasis in *Phase II* (Lessons 41-125) is on word clusters rather than single words, which students volunteer and the teacher writes, although single words can be written on the chart. During Phase II, for example, if a student volunteers *flag*, you might ask, "What kind of flag?" and the student might reply, *"United States flag."* You then write each letter of the cluster, *United States flag*, spelling each letter as it is written with class members joining in—*Capital U-n-i-t-e-d Capital S-t-a-t-e-s f-l-a-g*. Students are learning the concept of word groupings. If the student cannot think of an adjective or other words related to *flag*, the teacher writes the single word *flag* on the chart paper. The example of a chart from Lesson 46 (Figure 2-3) is from Phase II. Note the word clusters *table top*, *crunchy cereal*, and *big ears* as well as the single words *tongue*, *food*, and *bowl*.

The following is an example of the difference in Phase I and Phase II:

During Phase I, a student might point to a part of a picture and say *table* and you would record the word *table* saying each letter aloud as you write it and asking any members of the class who would like to join you in saying of the names of the letters to do so. During Phase II, however, if a student volunteered the word *table*, you would say, "Tell me something about the table," or "What color is the table?" to encourage the student to volunteer more than the one word *table*. If the student responds with *tall table*, *antique table*, or *cream-colored table*, you record those words, again saying each letter as you write it with members of the class who recognize the letters joining in. Students are learning how groups of words are written.

The following happened in one *Success* class:

> A child noticed the space between the two words *electric stove* and asked why the teacher had left the space. The teacher

I II III
words - clusters - sentences

pronounced the words, pausing between each to illustrate that the vocal pause was one way to distinguish between words, and a space between letters was another way of showing when one word stopped and another began. The child immediately grasped the concept. Most of the students had already learned this concept; for this child, it happened during Phase II.

Phase III incorporates Lessons 126–180. During this Phase each chart should contain at least one *sentence.* Although single words and word clusters can be written on the chart, you should expand a student's response until it becomes a sentence. It is within these sentences and some of the word clusters that the traditional "sight words" such as *and, is, when,* and *for* are introduced and students learn to read and spell them. One major difference between the *Success* program and some other programs is that sight words are used in context, never in isolation or in drills.

Preliminary work with sentence composing begun during Lesson 20 will help students expand their use of sentences during Phase III. This Phase also expands the depth and scope of the reading/writing association process.

In Phase III, as in the preceding phases, *the teacher should say the name of each letter as it is written* on the chart paper. Students should be encouraged, but not pressured or required, to say letters they know or hear. Gradually, most students learn to spell key letter components within words.

During Phase III, there will definitely be several students who will be able to and want to write on the chart paper instead of watching you write.

When a sentence is volunteered earlier in the year, you should record the complete sentence, ad-lib about the first letter in a sentence starting with a capital letter and the kind of punctuation mark used, and note that this is a complete sentence. The difference among the three Phases is on the *emphasis*—words to clusters of words to sentences. During Phase III, all recordings do not have to be sentences—single words and word clusters can be recorded; however, towards the end of the year there should be more sentences than clusters. Time will not permit writing one sentence volunteered by *each* student each day in this part of the lesson. You will need to be selective with the words included in the writing. Every word spoken by the student does not need to be written.

The question is frequently asked if the words on the charts are used in class after the chart is completed or if students should learn words on the charts. There is never any formal use of the charts after the module is completed for the day, although students themselves may refer to the charts in various informal ways. The charts provide a dramatic and educationally sound vehicle for students to learn the reading/writing *process.* The object is not to zero in on a few words out of the thousands in the English language and try to get students to learn to spell or read them. Most of the words they volunteer will be encountered many, many times during their lives. The Picture/Word Association Module introduces students not only to how words are formed, but also illustrates that *how* words are used affects their interpretation.

There are no formal reviews and drills, but rather the development of hundreds of words during the Picture/Word Association Modules throughout the year. Most students learn to read many words and spell most of the letters in correct sequence within the words. With the exception of obscene or generally offensive words, there is no controlled vocabulary in the *Success* program.

SELECTED SUBTHEMES

In addition to providing opportunities for students to observe the reading/writing process each day of the year, the topics suggested for selecting pictures to use in this module and therefore for discussion by the students, provide fantastic springboards for both introduction to new knowledge areas and contributions by students about topics with which they are familiar.

One question that arose while researching and piloting this module was whether a unit model should be followed. For example, if the unit was animals, then for several consecutive days the pictures used in this module would pertain to different animals, their habits, environments, etc., before moving to a new unit theme. Some teachers preferred this type of sequence or selected pictures to accompany a theme being studied at other times during the day.

Other teachers wanted to change the picture emphasis each day to a different topic, encouraging a wide variety of discussions and avoiding the possibility of children becoming bored with too much repetition of the same theme. In the Picture/Word Association Modules in Appendix One, the picture themes are changed *daily* instead of following the unit plan. If teachers of the *Success* program prefer to follow a unit plan, they should rearrange picture topics by writing those topics on the module plan in Appendix One. For example, if the first unit is about *animals*, the teacher might use the suggestions in the first column in Lessons 2, 28, 33, 39, 106, 110, 129, or 130 which deal with different animals, or substitute some of the animals suggested for other animals. Those topics would then be the emphasis in Lessons 1–8 instead of the ones suggested.

The important points are to use at least one picture each day in the Picture/Word Association Module and to cover as many topics as possible during the academic year.

Following is a list of seventeen units one kindergarten teacher used during the academic year. The Picture/Word Association Module themes found in Appendix One were correlated with the unit topics, and the unit itself was emphasized at a different time during the day.

1. Safety
2. Fall
3. Community helpers
4. The senses
5. Winter
6. Dinosaurs
7. Transportation
8. Outer space
9. Animals
10. Circus
11. Pollution
12. Parts of the body
13. Spring
14. Insects
15. Seeds
16. Energy
17. Summer

Figures 2–4, 2–5, and 2–6 are examples of how one kindergarten teacher chose to change the topics suggested in Lessons 1, 2, and 3. On day one, a "gingerbread hunt" was conducted as a means of familiarizing various parts of the school building to the students; hence, the theme "gingerbread man" was substituted for the suggested theme, "face" (see Figure 2-4).

Teaching "safety" was required during the first week in the school. Therefore, the theme "school bus" was used for Lesson 2 rather than the suggested theme of "animals" on day two. The teacher drew a picture of a school bus on the chart paper and the students volunteered words relating to the picture. Note the inclusion of word clusters as well as single words (see Figure 2-5).

On day three, the kindergarten class acquired some gerbils. The teacher decided to use *gerbils* as the theme for the Picture/Word Association Module for Lesson 3 rather than the suggested theme, "buildings." The teacher drew a picture of a gerbil cage and the students volunteered words related to the picture. Note the correlation of the Alphabet Module with mathematics. The teacher decided to write sentences as well as single words (see Figure 2-6).

Table 2–1 lists the subthemes in selected areas of emphasis in the Picture/Word Association Module. The list should be helpful to teachers in planning for instruction, especially if they adopt the unit plan, and it is useful in parent-teacher conferences to indicate some of the items that children in the class will have opportunities to explore in this module during the year.

SELECTION OF PICTORIAL AIDS

The general guide for selecting pictures is to choose pictures that are distinct, clear, and that contain details. Magazine pictures should be used frequently, but not exclusively in the Picture/Word Association Module. You can use pictures from calendars, posters, napkins, and pages in catalogues. Because of the quality of newsprint, most newspaper pictures are not distinct enough to use; however, occasionally one might be found that is suitable. For some modules, draw the picture yourself—even if you do not consider yourself an artist—and the students can volunteer items they would like you to add to the drawing. Somehow the imagination of the children compensates for teachers who are not overly artistic. On some days,

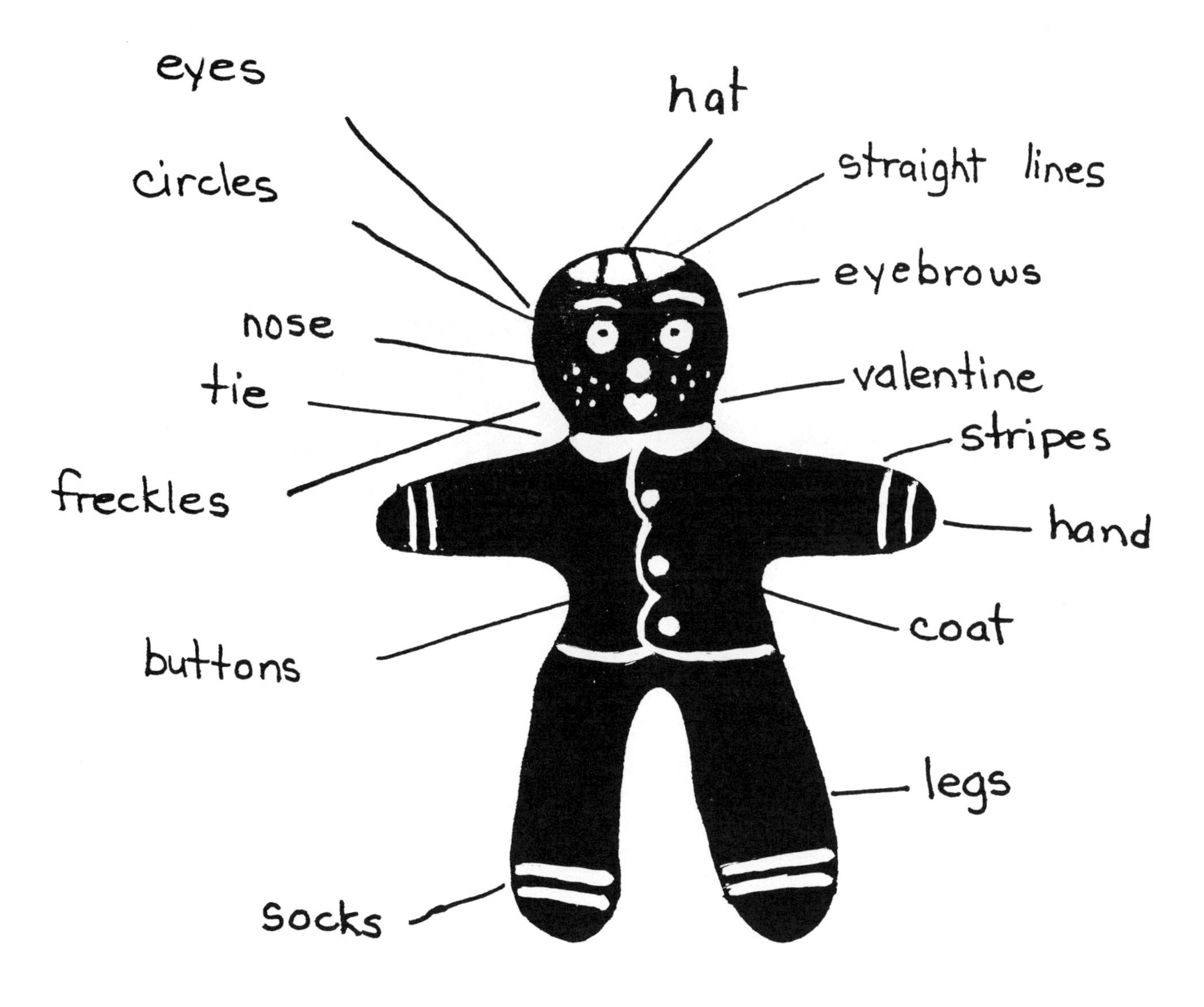

FIGURE 2–4 **Chart Theme Substituted by Teacher for Lesson 1**

you should ask each student to draw some small part of a class-developed picture. Teachers have used one side of a toy box-top in this module. The pictorial aid does not have to be limited to pictures only.

Avoid constantly using "artificially pretty," so-called educational pictures that are sold commercially for use in preschool and primary classes. One important aspect of this module is to bring reality based pictures into the kindergarten program.

TANGIBLE AND INTANGIBLE CONCEPTS

Although many of the students' responses will be associated directly with tangible items in the pictures, such as *car*, *airplane*, or *glasses*, a surprising number of responses are not direct. For example, if one part of the picture is a circle, students may make responses such as found in Figure 2-7.

Do not limit students to concrete words for items. Encourage their expression of intangible or association concepts.

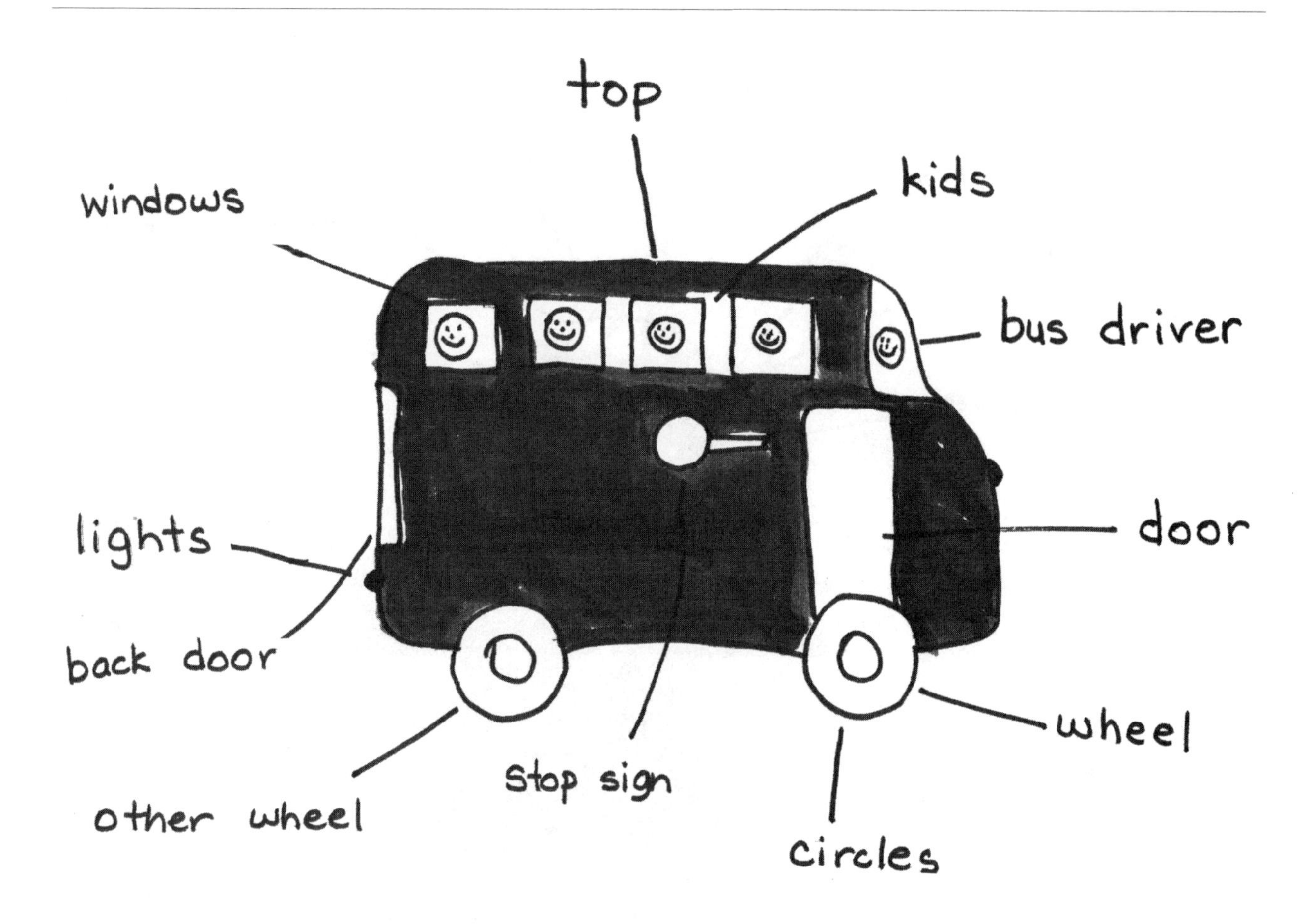

FIGURE 2–5 **Chart Theme Substituted by Teacher for Lesson 2**

It is important that all students be in the group seated before the chart each day. Do not repeat the procedure of teaching this module with small groups; it will be physically draining on you. Within a fairly short amount of time all students can participate with the total class. It is damaging to separate or segregate students and stereotype them because they cannot accomplish a task at one particular interval in their educational growth. Keep all students with the same group in this module and give them all a chance to learn to work with others as well as to do something within the activity themselves.

Simple courtesy and listening skills should be taught during this module each day. Students should learn to raise their hands and listen to the one who is speaking. It should not be a pandemonium module, nor should it be squelched. There is time for each student to have a turn at the chart and many turns speaking. When conducted in this manner, the Picture/Word Association Module is one of the most enjoyable of the day for teacher and students. It is important that this module not be skipped.

Today we found 4 t's.

Today we found 4 l's.

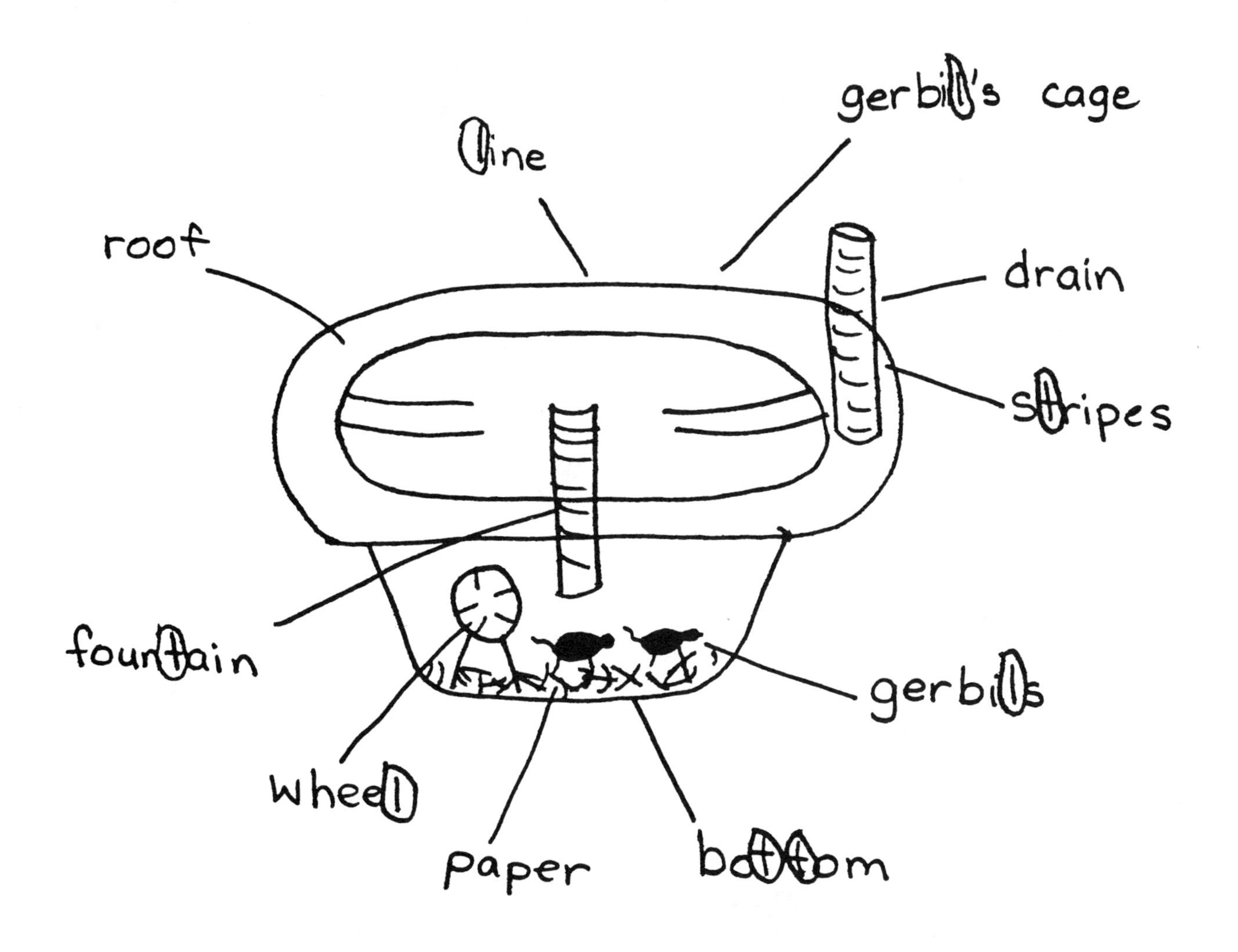

FIGURE 2-6 **Chart Theme Substituted by Teacher for Lesson 3**

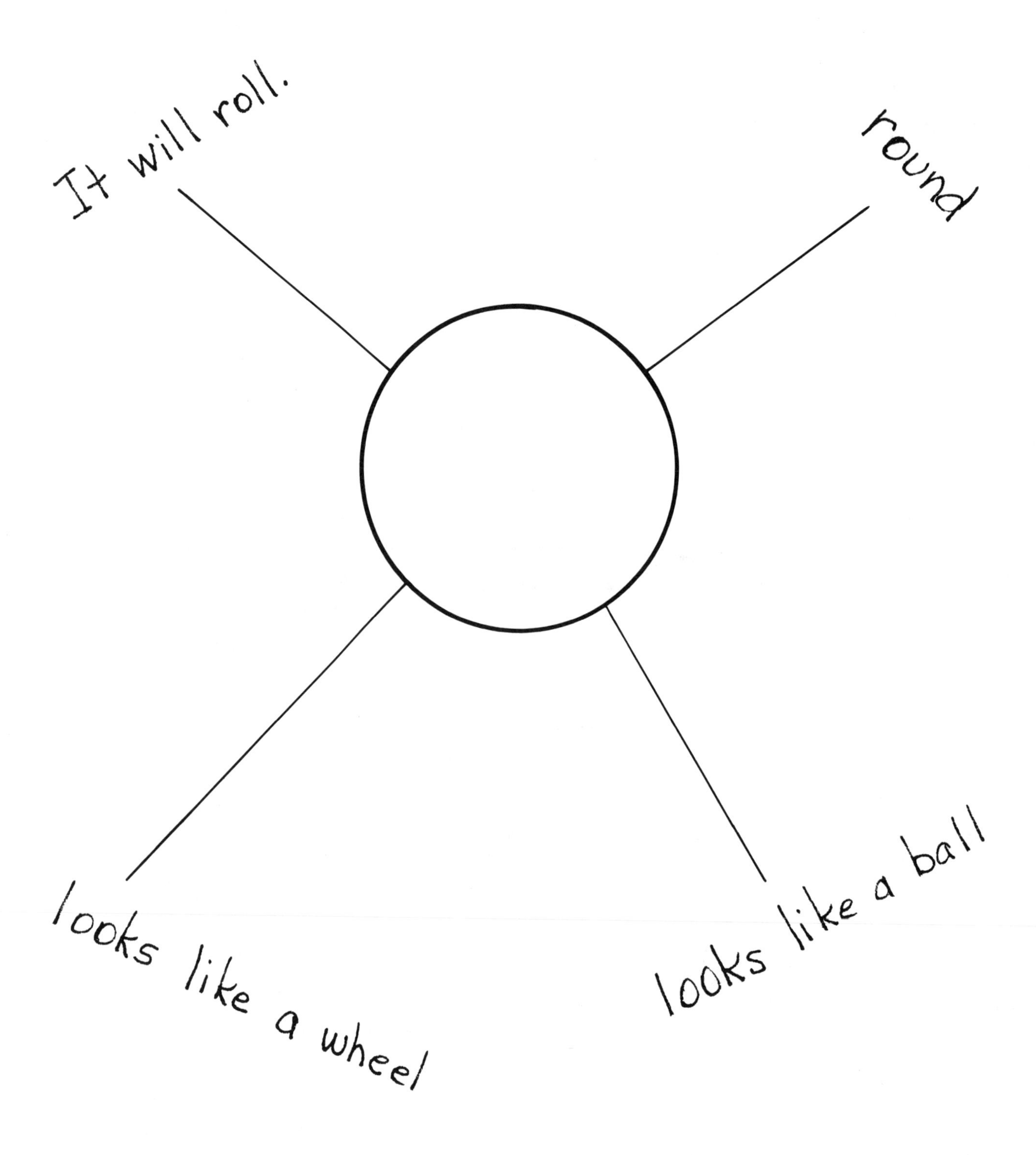

FIGURE 2-7

TABLE 2–1 Selected Emphases Areas in the Picture/Word Association Module
(Pictures should be selected that deal with these areas or concepts.)

People	Animals	Objects		Places	Food	Environment	Parts of the Body	Geometry	Senses	Seasons
story characters	horses	furniture	boxes	buildings	vegetables	rain	eyes	squares	smell	winter
firefighters	snakes	automobiles	metals	kitchens	meats	snow	ears	rectangles	feeling	summer
physicians	cows	money	toys	street intersections	fruits	water	hair	circles	hearing	spring
sanitation workers	dogs	teeth	Frisbees	table tops	fish	trees	feet	lines	taste	fall
police officers	outdoor animals	sweaters	motorcycles	rivers	sandwiches	landscapes	fingers		seeing	
teachers	indoor animals	lawnmowers	puzzles	sky	bubble gum	fire				
dentists	insects	airplanes	tennis shoes	stairs	hamburgers	crops				
parents	turtles	chairs	radios	mountains	jelly beans	stars				
athletes	rabbits	bicycles	tractors	streets	hot dogs	fog				
scientists	apes	desks	sandboxes	houses	ice cream	deserts				
senators	parrots	walls	tents	woods	strawberries	plants				
astronauts	ants	eyes	nickles	shops	carrots	cactus				
crowds	pigs	papers	sticks	cities	cereals	rainbows				
television stars	bears	boats	bandages	hills	peanut butter	oceans				
queens	gerbils	clothes	boats	ponds		rocks				
witches	frogs	stones	medicine	beaches						
cartoon characters	fish	tools	hats	bus stations						
fairy godmothers	mice	lights	fences	airport terminals						
race car drivers		floors		drug stores						
basketball players				grocery stores						
princes				baseball fields						
kings				schools						
football players										
presidents										
boxers										
grandparents										
clowns										
custodians										
principals										
children										

chapter three

How to Teach the Alphabet Module

The purposes of the Alphabet Module include introducing students to writing symbols of the English language, and the noting of selected sounds of letter combinations in ways that are correlated with language development, art, object association, listening, and rhyming.

The Alphabet Module is the second 20 minutes of each lesson. Refer to the third column in Appendix One for suggested sequences and emphases. The kindergarten teachers who piloted the *Success* program recommended that the Alphabet Module either follow directly after the Picture/Word Association Module, or come after "free play" following the Picture/Word Association Module.

Throughout the years few people have objected to pre-first graders using crayons to color or pencils to draw. However, some people wanted to draw the line as far as students writing alphabet letters or words until they were safely tucked into the first grade. The same people who advocated coloring as a device to help improve fine muscle coordination did not extend their theory to include writing letters with a pencil. As stated in the Preface to this book, the *Success* program avoids the controversy and affords classroom situations for those students who want to write letters and words to be able to do so. Other students can color or do other artwork during the same instructional time.

The elements of pressure are removed from this program. No student should be "made" to form an alphabet symbol correctly or "draw" an adult rendition of a horse; however, they can be helped to create a part of a letter or a part of a horse.

Correlating the writing activities with art provides a merger of the old and the new. The result is a much stronger kindergarten program that allows for the concept of readiness and extends beyond "getting ready to write" to getting ready to write the next set of written symbols the students want to write.

Combining art and the writing of letters, words, word clusters, and sentences pertaining to an art theme also helps save money on paper. This is significant in schools where limited budgets have reduced paper supplies for kindergarten classes. Another advantage is teaching the concept that words can be associated with students' drawings as well as with commercial drawings and pictures drawn by adults.

MATERIALS FOR THE ALPHABET MODULE

No chart paper is used in the Alphabet Module. The following materials are needed:

chalkboard
chalk
one sheet of *unlined* paper per student each day
regular-sized pencils with erasers
crayons
one manila folder per student
a cardboard box to hold the manila folders
newspapers
magazines

Only after an *individual* student can form letter symbols with legibility and has developed the concept of spacing between letters and words should lined paper be introduced, and then only to that particular student.

Students who could not make a letter or anything remotely resembling a letter early in the year will probably be writing legibly by the end of the year if the sequence is followed in the Alphabet Module, and each student receives assistance from the teacher every day. The guideline to use in helping students to write is to comment positively on some part of a letter attempted and show how some part could be improved. Do not adopt a sense of urgency for an individual to suddenly become proficient in letter formation—there is plenty of time. It is best if the students enjoy *trying* to make the letter symbols than worry about pleasing the teacher.

Suppose you were to learn to write a new "letter symbol" and your teacher insisted you write as perfectly as possible to the original "new" letter:

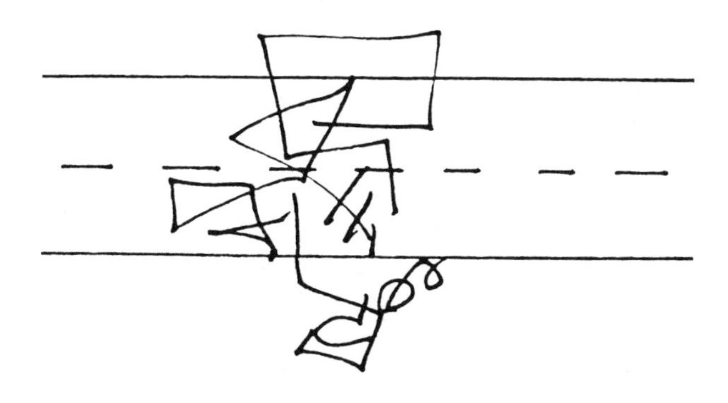

If your teacher gave you enough time, help, and encouragement, and *if you wanted to learn to write the letter* as it was supposed to be written correctly, you would do so. By correlating the writing of letters with art activities, students have a chance to enjoy learning to write and to improve their writing abilities.

Most of the kindergarten students in the pilot *Success* classes were writing with legibility by the end of the year. When the teacher leaned over a student's paper and helped with some, but not *every* letter on that paper, the student had a chance to observe and respond. Whole class writing of the same letter in the same mold at the same minute is not included in this program.

Although the major materials used in the Alphabet Module are crayons, pencils, and unlined paper, there are classes where ditto stencils and coloring books are used. Extensive use of ditto stencil copy is extremely limiting and restricting. The primary advantage of predrawn pictures is the inclusion of line drawings to help students develop spatial awareness and small muscle coordination as they learn to correlate their markings with the design. If a stencil copy is used, it should be on rare occasions. Student drawings on paper should be encouraged in the majority of the Alphabet Modules.

A few decades ago someone invented the "big pencil." Even though it was heavier, unwieldly, and in general harder to use by small hands, the "big pencil" found its way into thousands of classrooms. These kinds of pencils are not recommended for use in the *Success* program. Use regular pencils with erasers. Even kindergartners want to do "real writing" with "real pencils."

HOW TO TEACH THE ALPHABET MODULE

There are three distinct parts of each Alphabet Module, no matter what time of year the module is taught or which symbols or kinds of words are emphasized within the module.

The Alphabet Module begins each day with the teacher at the chalkboard and the students with their paper, crayons, and pencils. The procedure of teaching the module is basically the same each day. On the first day of the *Success* program, teach the first lesson in the Alphabet Module. On the second day, teach the second lesson in the Alphabet Module. Continue the procedure throughout the year.

Do not repeat the same letter emphasis for more than one day consecutively. That letter will continue to reappear throughout the rest of the student's life. Although the temptation to keep teaching the same letter until all students can write it legibly may be great, it is not an educationally sound practice to follow. On an individual basis, you can help students form letters at their desks while other students perform more advanced writing.

Part One of the Alphabet Module

Introduce the module emphasis to the entire class by writing examples on the chalkboard and explaining letter or word formations. Give both the art and letter or word writing directions to the class. This is a part of the built-in listening aspect of the Alphabet Module within the total *Success* program.

Part Two of the Alphabet Module

Each student writes, draws, or colors at a desk or table, completing the activity according to his or her ability. You should move from student to student making positive comments and giving assistance to each individual *at least twice* each day during the Alphabet Module. There is a developmental sequence of activities as the year progresses and as new Phases are taught.

During this part of the Alphabet Module, each student develops letters and/or words, depending on the Phase under way, as well as the artwork involved. Early in the year, they will learn to write or improve their writing. Later in the year, for example during Phase IV, they will make their own flash cards for items in the classroom.

Part Three of the Alphabet Module

Each student's paper is dated and filed each day in a manila folder with the student's name on it. The alphabetized folders are kept in a box labeled *Alphabet Module Papers*, and the papers* in the folder are not sent home until the end of the school year. Papers from other parts of the school day should be sent home, depending on your directions; however, by keeping the papers developed each day during the Alphabet Module, you have a longitudinal record of the progress of each individual student in the class. These folders are extremely helpful in parent-teacher conferences and in teacher assessment of individual student progress.

Figures 3-1, 3-2, and 3-3 are examples of three kindergarten students' work at different times during the academic year. Note the progress of each student.

Dating the papers is extremely important. At first, the teacher will need to date each paper, for example, "9-4-80;" however many students learn to do this fairly early in the year. You should put the date on the chalkboard each school day. Use numerals—do not ask students to consume the time needed to write the name of the month.

There is a specific emphasis within *each* Alphabet Module. The sequence of emphases within the module is designed to help students begin writing and/or improve their writing; however, the sequence can be changed at your discretion.

*Each student should have opportunities each day to make pencil or crayon notations, letters and/or words on a sheet of paper which is dated and filed. The object is recognition of effort, not mastery of product.

USE OF NEWSPAPERS AND MAGAZINES

Every fifth lesson in the Alphabet Module beginning with Lesson 1 and continuing through Lesson 72 includes the use of newspapers and/or magazines.

The use of newspapers and magazines provides activities for kindergarten students that offer variety and exposure to everyday reading material. Figures 3-4 through 3-7 are examples of how newspapers can be used in the Alphabet Module. Figure 3-4 shows the letter *b* circled (Lesson 10); Figure 3-5 shows the letter *u* circled (Lesson 15); Figure 3-6 shows the letter *E* circled (Lesson 46); and Figure 3-7 shows the letter cluster *th* circled (Lesson 65).

As indicated in the examples, you should direct students to tear or cut sections from the newspaper, paste them on paper, and circle or underline the specific letter(s).

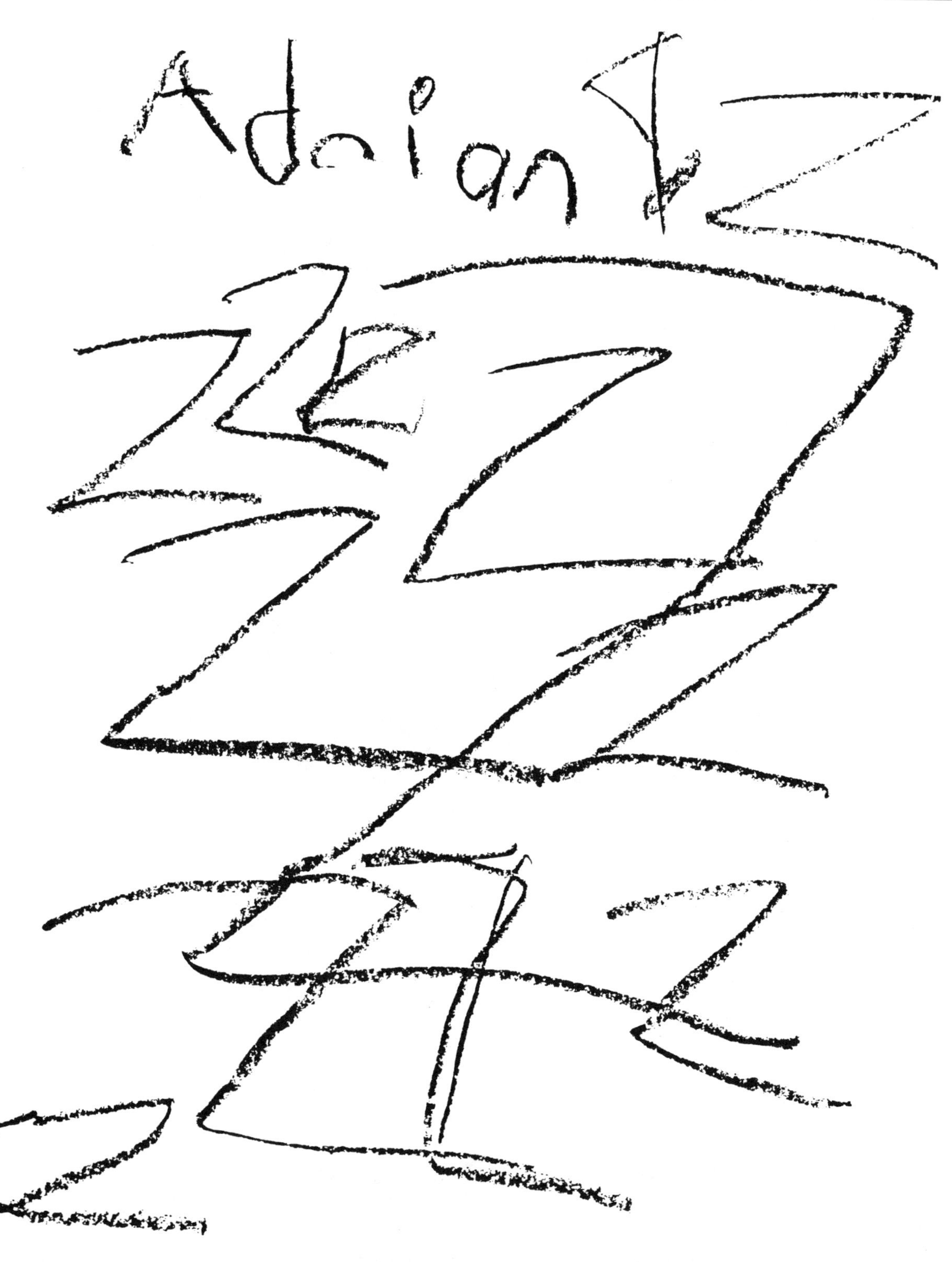

FIGURE 3-1 Example of Student One's Paper—Alphabet Module, Lesson 16

FIGURE 3–1 Example of Student One's Paper—Alphabet Module, Lesson 21 (continued)

FIGURE 3-1 Example of Student One's Paper—Alphabet Module, Lesson 23 (continued)

FIGURE 3-1 Example of Student One's Paper—Alphabet Module, Lesson 50 (continued)

FIGURE 3-1 Example of Student One's Paper—Alphabet Module, Lesson 76 (continued)

FIGURE 3-1 Example of Student One's Paper—Alphabet Module, Lesson 180 (continued)

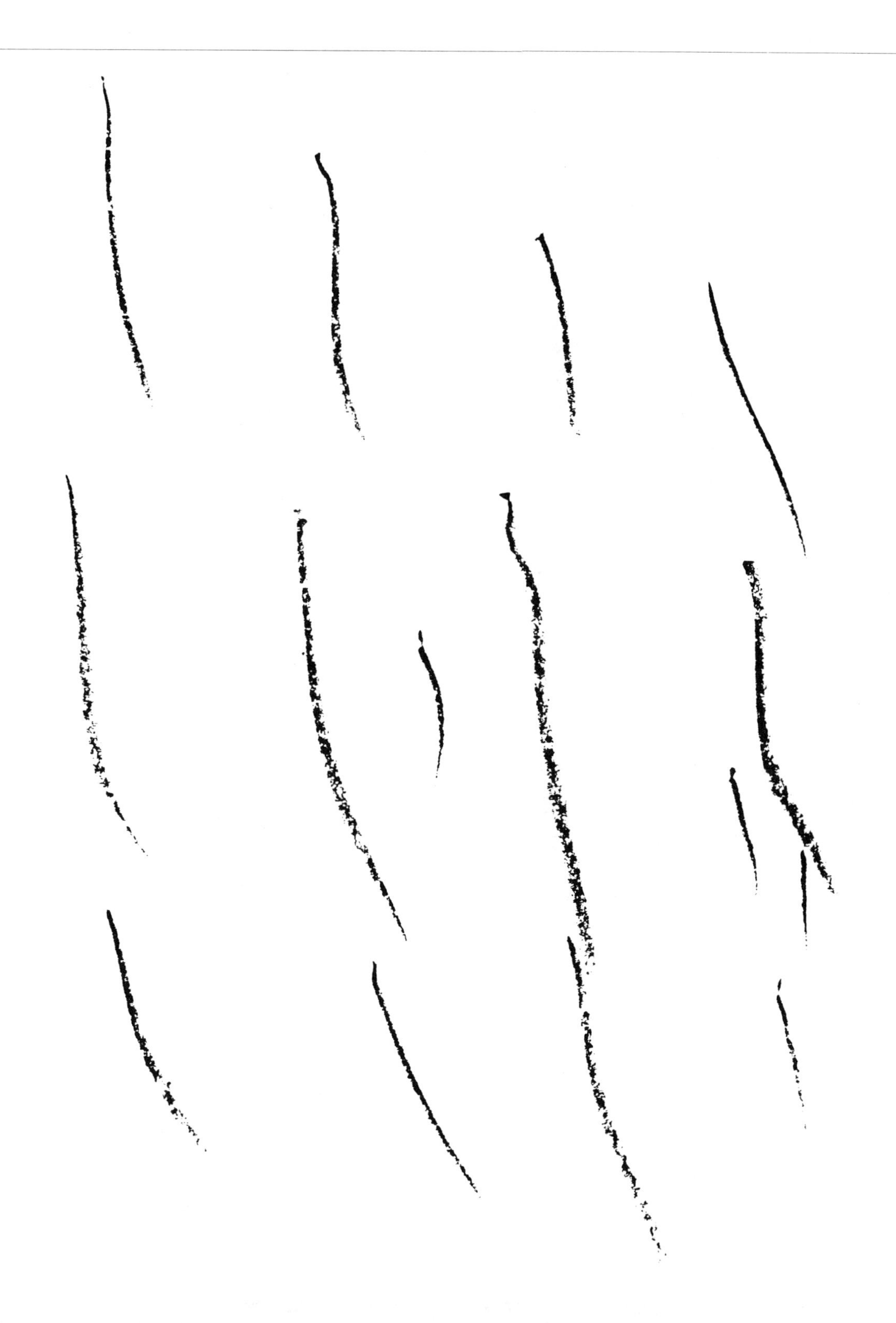

FIGURE 3-2 Example of Student Two's Paper—Alphabet Module, Lesson 1

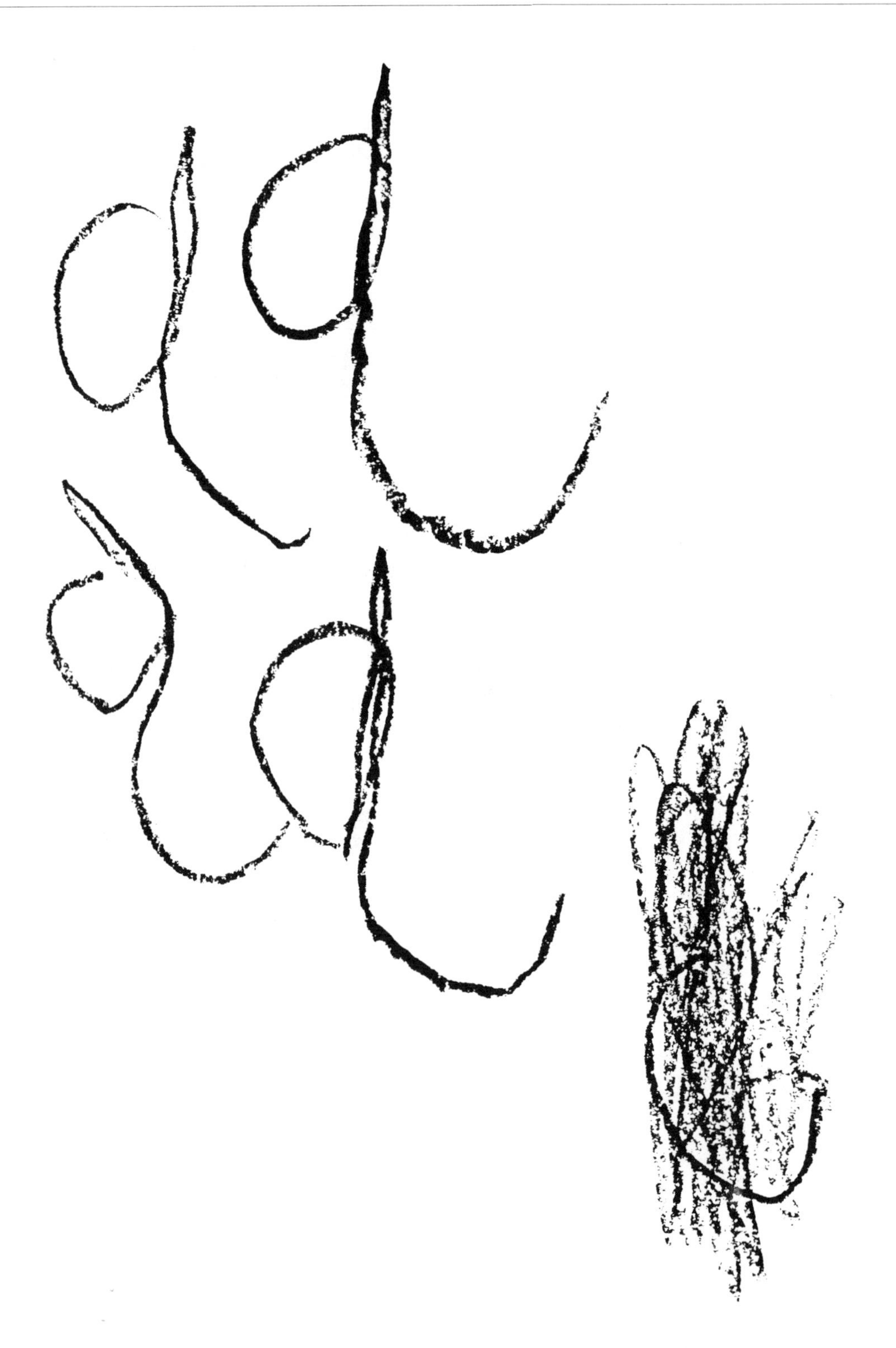

FIGURE 3-2 Example of Student Two's Paper—Alphabet Module, Lesson 26 (continued)

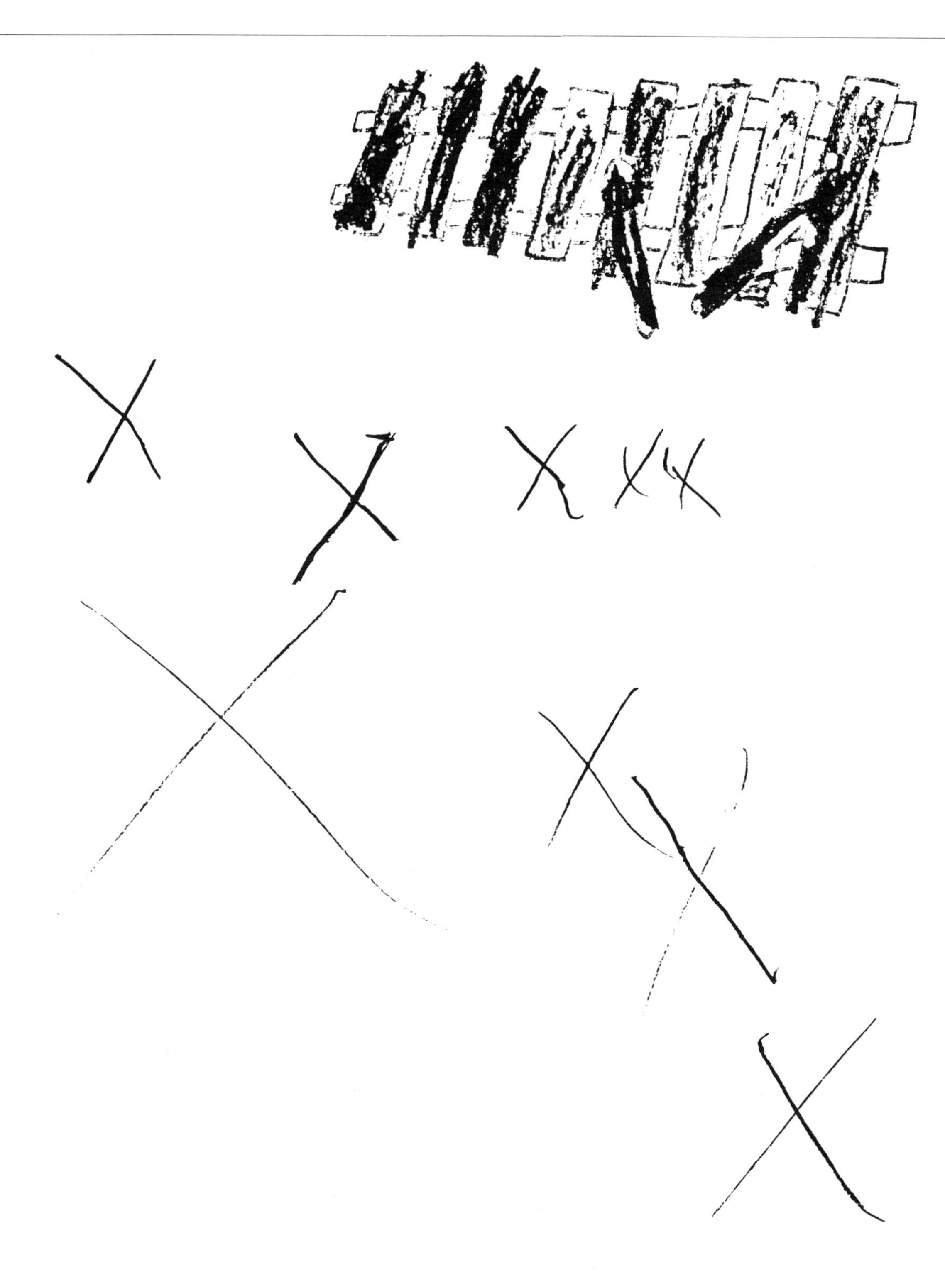

FIGURE 3-2 Example of Student Two's Paper—Alphabet Module, Lesson 37 (continued)

FIGURE 3–2 Example of Student Two's Paper—Alphabet Module, Lesson 93 (continued)

FIGURE 3-2 **Example of Student Two's Paper—Alphabet Module, Lesson 155 (continued)**

FIGURE 3-3 Example of Student Three's Paper—Alphabet Module, Lesson 13

FIGURE 3–3 Example of Student Three's Paper—Alphabet Module, Lesson 16 (continued)

FIGURE 3-3 Example of Student Three's Paper—Alphabet Module, Lesson 21 (continued)

FIGURE 3–3 Example of Student Three's Paper—Alphabet Module, Lesson 82 (continued)

The News and Observer

FIGURE 3-4 Example of Kindergarten Student Circling Letter *b* in Newspaper—Lesson 10, Alphabet Module

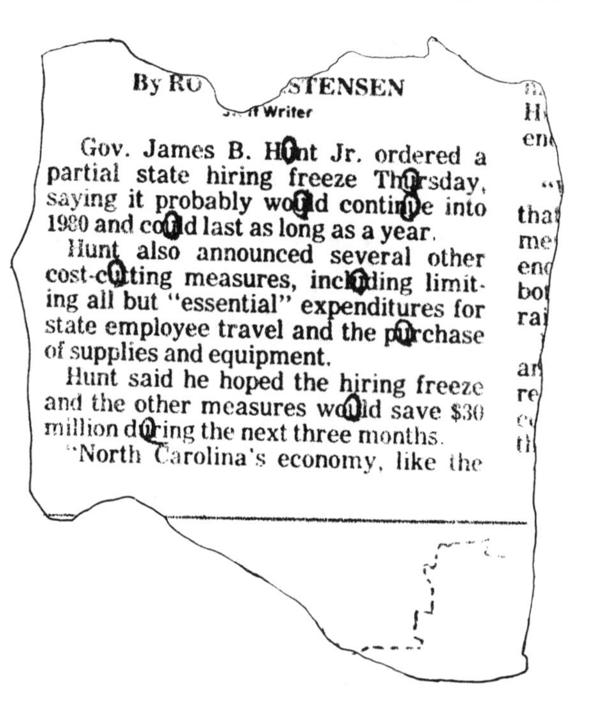

By RO STENSEN
Writer

Gov. James B. Hunt Jr. ordered a partial state hiring freeze Thursday, saying it probably would continue into 1980 and could last as long as a year.

Hunt also announced several other cost-cutting measures, including limiting all but "essential" expenditures for state employee travel and the purchase of supplies and equipment.

Hunt said he hoped the hiring freeze and the other measures would save $30 million during the next three months.

"North Carolina's economy, like the

FIGURE 3-5 Example of Kindergarten Student Circling Letter *u* —Lesson 15, Alphabet Module

FIGURE 3-6 Example of Kindergarten Student Circling Letter *E* in Newspaper—Lesson 46, Alphabet Module

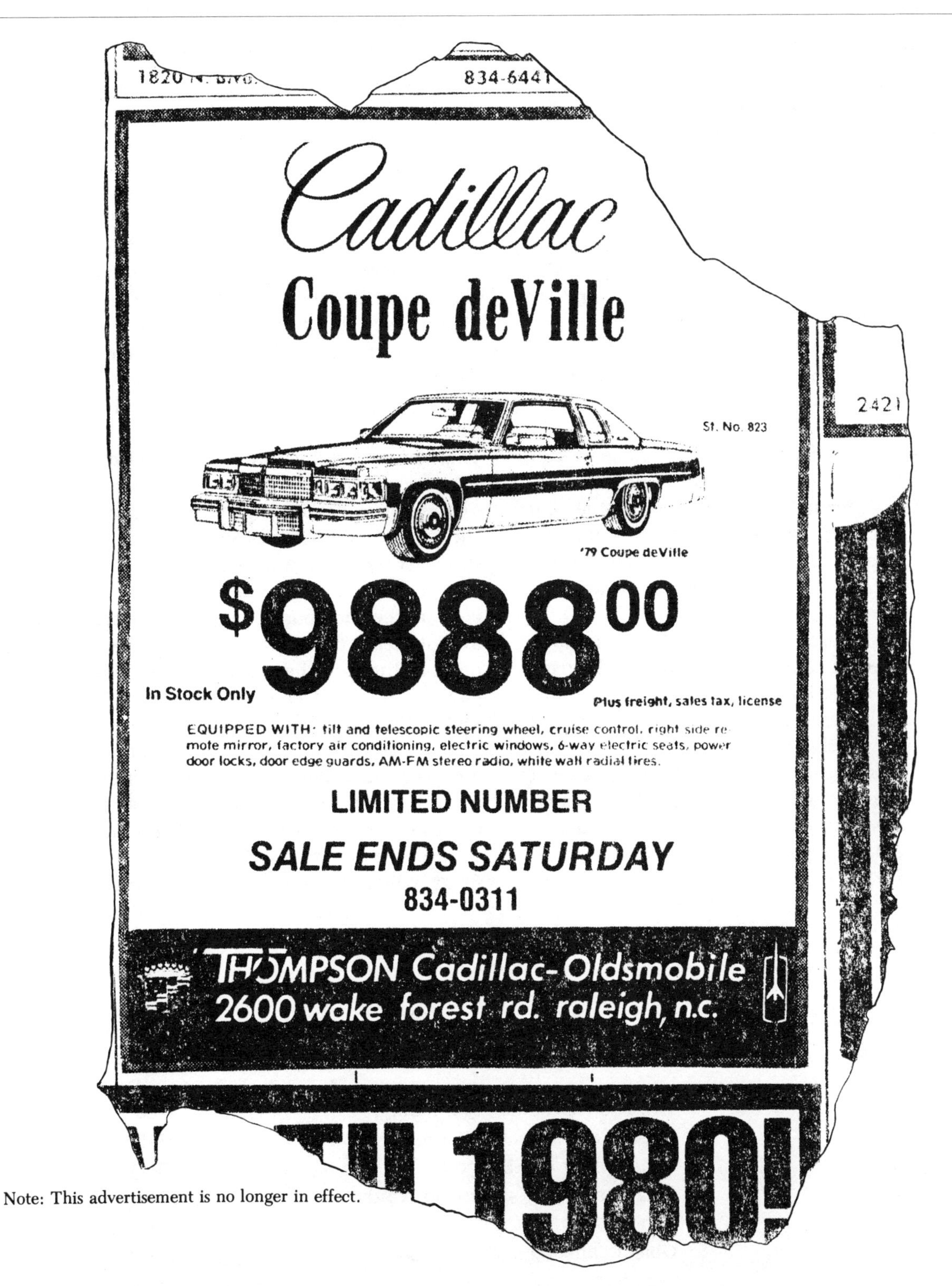

Note: This advertisement is no longer in effect.

FIGURE 3-7 **Example of Kindergarten Student Circling Letter Cluster *th* in Newspaper—Lesson 65, Alphabet Module**

THE DEVELOPMENTAL PHASES WITHIN THE ACADEMIC YEAR

Although the basic format found in the preceding section should be followed to teach each Alphabet Module, the content *within* these modules changes as the year progresses.

There are eight developmental Phases in the Alphabet Module. Each Phase contains a different approach to introduce students to writing. Table 3-1 is a list of the emphasis in each Phase and the lessons where the emphasis is found.

Although each Phase has an emphasis, all students should not be expected to achieve *mastery*. For example, some students will not learn to write lower case alphabet symbols during Phase I, while in the same classroom other students will be writing single letters as well as using them in various positions in words during the same Phase. As the year progresses, however, most students become increasingly comfortable about writing symbols of the alphabet both in isolation and in contextual situations.

Refer to Figures 3-8, 3-9, and 3-10, examples of three different students' papers completed during Lesson 15 of the Alphabet Module in the same classroom on the same day. Note the wide range of abilities evident within the same classroom. Student One was beginning to form the letter *u;* student Two wrote the letter *u* legibly; student Three wrote her own words containing the letter *u*. The *Success* program provides opportunities for all students to work according to their capabilities.

Guidelines for Teaching Phase I Lower Case Letters, Lessons 1-26

During Phase I, the first 26 days of the *Success* program, the emphasis is on providing opportunities for students to practice letter formations, using pencils. Only lower case letters are included in Phase I. A different letter is emphasized *each day*. Lower case alphabet letters are placed first in the sequence of the 180 days of the Alphabet Module because more students are familiar with lower case letters than with upper case or capital letters.

The sequence of letters in this module is from the easiest to form to the more difficult letters. Look at the Alphabet Module in Lesson 1. The first letter, and the easiest to write is *l*. The first 26 modules emphasize writing lower case letters. Do not introduce upper case letters until Lesson 27. Several of the letters have completely different strokes for the upper and lower cases, and others have different sizes of the same letter shape.

1. Make a large letter (for Lesson 1, the letter is *l*), on the chalkboard and trace the symbol in the air. Students trace the symbol in the air at their desks as they say the name of the symbol. Students can also make letter formations with their fingers and with their bodies. Two of the authors visited one kindergarten class during Lesson 15 and observed the students on the floor forming the letter *u* with their bodies. This part of the module correlates letter formation with physical activity. Some of the pilot teachers and their students created songs which were sung during this part of the

TABLE 3-1

Phase	Content Emphasis	Lessons
I	Lower Case Alphabet Formation	1-26
II	Upper Case Alphabet Formation	27-52
III	Initial Patterning Sounds	53-72
IV	Final Patterning—Rhyming Words	73-100
V	Various Vowels	101-120
VI	Object Labeling in the Classroom	121-130
VII	Dictation	131-154
VIII	Consonant Completion	155-180

FIGURE 3-8 Example of Student One's Paper—Alphabet Module, Lesson 15

FIGURE 3–9 Example of Student Two's Paper—Alphabet Module, Lesson 15

FIGURE 3–10 Example of Student Three's Paper—Alphabet Module, Lesson 15

module, thereby correlating music with physical activity. On the majority of days when the students draw during this module, you may wish to draw a model on the chalkboard. An item to draw is suggested in the first 26 modules. You may wish to draw something other than the suggested item. Your artistic abilities do not seem to matter to the students. For example, during the first module, you could draw a ladder on the chalkboard, and write some *l*'s near or on it (see Figure 3-11).

FIGURE 3-11 Example of a Teacher-Drawn Ladder with *l*'s Around And On It

2. Children use crayons or pencils for the remainder of the module to draw and/or color a picture. In Lesson 1, it could be a ladder or any other item. The art item does *not* have to begin with the letter emphasized for writing, although it is preferred that a *l* be somewhere in the word. The major objective is providing time for students to practice writing *l*'s and providing time for artwork.

Do not insist that each student draw the same picture. Do not be concerned if the students' drawings do not remotely resemble the topic. The only requirement is that they write as many of the module's suggested letter(s) as they would like to on or beside the drawing, or on the paper. The back of the paper is used for additional artwork or practice of writing letter(s) if the student wishes to do so.

Figure 3-12 is an example of a kindergarten student's paper from another *Success* classroom. The paper was developed during Lesson 1, and this figure represents the front of the paper.

Figure 3-14 is an example of a kindergarten student's paper developed during Lesson 2 where the letter emphasis was *t*. In this particular classroom, the teacher provided a stencil copy of the drawing. The student colored the front side of the paper and practiced writing *t*'s on the back side of the sheet (Figure 3-15).

Especially at the beginning of the year, there may be little resemblance between the student writing and the symbol's shape; however, kindergarten teachers noted that improvement in writing was observed during the year for all students. Figure 3-16 is an example of a kindergarten student's making the letter *g* on the 24th day of the program during Lesson 24. Mastery of each letter is *not* a requirement. Each student writes the letter on or beside the artwork during this module, or on the back of the page. Artwork at other times during the day, of course, does not necessarily have the component of writing letters/words.

The students create some very interesting designs writing the letters. Note the example of the Alphabet Module for Lesson 24 in Figure 3-16. In that particular class the picture had been predrawn. The student made the g's and colored the picture during the module time. Some students created only part of a g; some wrote only one or two g's; some wrote beautifully formed g's; some wrote numerous g's. It is important, as stated earlier, that a different letter should be emphasized on the following day.

You should not attempt to have the student make every letter as perfect as possible. The students simply enjoy writing the letters as a form of art. They place the letters on the unlined paper wherever they like, and they make as many letters as they like. All should try to make some part of a letter (with assistance from you) before the papers are filed, however

3. Date each students' paper and file it in a manila folder with the student's name. The folder should be alphabetized in a box labeled *Alphabet Module Papers.*

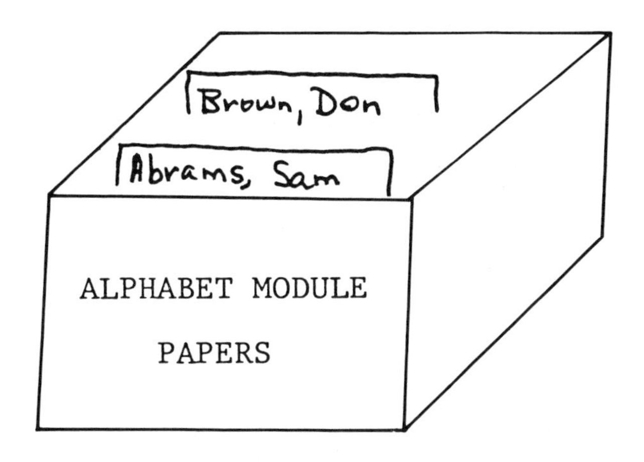

As students learn to file their own papers, they should be encouraged to do so. Do not send these papers home until the end of the year since they provide a longitudinal record of each student's progress. Papers written during other parts of the school day, as well as other artwork by the student may be sent home, depending on your directions.

Guidelines for Teaching Phase II—Upper Case Letters, Lessons 27-52

For the next 26 days, beginning with Lesson 27, write a different upper case letter at the chalkboard and have each student write it too during the art/writing part of this module. The procedure remains the same as in Phase I. It continues to be extremely important that you make a positive comment about the student's writing and, if necessary, assist each student at least *twice* each day during Phase II of the Alphabet Module.

There is no suggested art item for you to draw on the chalkboard during Phase II. The object is for students to create an upper case letter design each day around art drawings or on the back of the paper. It is not necessary that their artwork relate to a proper noun beginning with an upper case letter.

It is important that you teach this module each day and that you date and file each student's paper in the *Alphabet Module Papers* box. The date is extremely important. By the end of Phase II, many students can write their own first names and the date. You help only those students who cannot accomplish this basic procedure.

Refer to Figure 3-17, an example of a student's paper developed during Lesson 35. This figure represents the front of the paper where the student colored the rabbit. The back of the same paper is found in Figure 3-18, where the student practiced writing *B*'s. In another *Success* class on the same day, the teacher asked each student to make his or her own drawing; however, in both clases, students practiced forming *B*'s.

Guidelines for Teaching Phase III—Initial Patterning Sounds, Lessons 53-72

You should not infer that all students will have learned how to write letter symbols by the 53rd day of kindergarten. Rather you should continue to help students form alphabet symbols as they work with *words* that have the same initial pattern in Phase III.

Beginning with Phase III, Lesson 53, the emphasis in the Alphabet Module changes from letter formation to initial patterning sounds and the writing of the same first two or three letters in different words. There is no Phase on isolated initial consonant sounds because that sound can still be emphasized while immediately following with the sound of the next letter(s) in the word. The object is to introduce students to decoding sounds *together*, not making unnecessary breaks between sounds of letters within words. Although traditionally, single beginning consonant sounds have been emphasized in many readiness programs, the teachers of the *Success* kindergarten classes found it was much better to begin by emphasizing initial blend sounds.

The blend patterns selected for use in Phase III are considered minimum. The teacher may wish to add other blends or initial consonant clusters. Teach this Phase of the Alphabet Module in the following manner:

1. Write the pattern of letters found in the module Lesson on the chalkboard (or on chart paper if you wish to display the words for longer than a part of a day). In Lesson 53, for example, the initial pattern is *gr*, so you write *gr* on the chalkboard or on chart paper.

2. Pronounce the *sound* of the pattern rather than the letters *g,r*, and ask students to say the sound with you until someone thinks of a word that has the *gr* sound in it. Although most of the words will have the pattern in the initial position, some students may at times in this Phase volunteer words that have the pattern near the medial or ending of a word. Do not reject these words since they do contain the pattern.

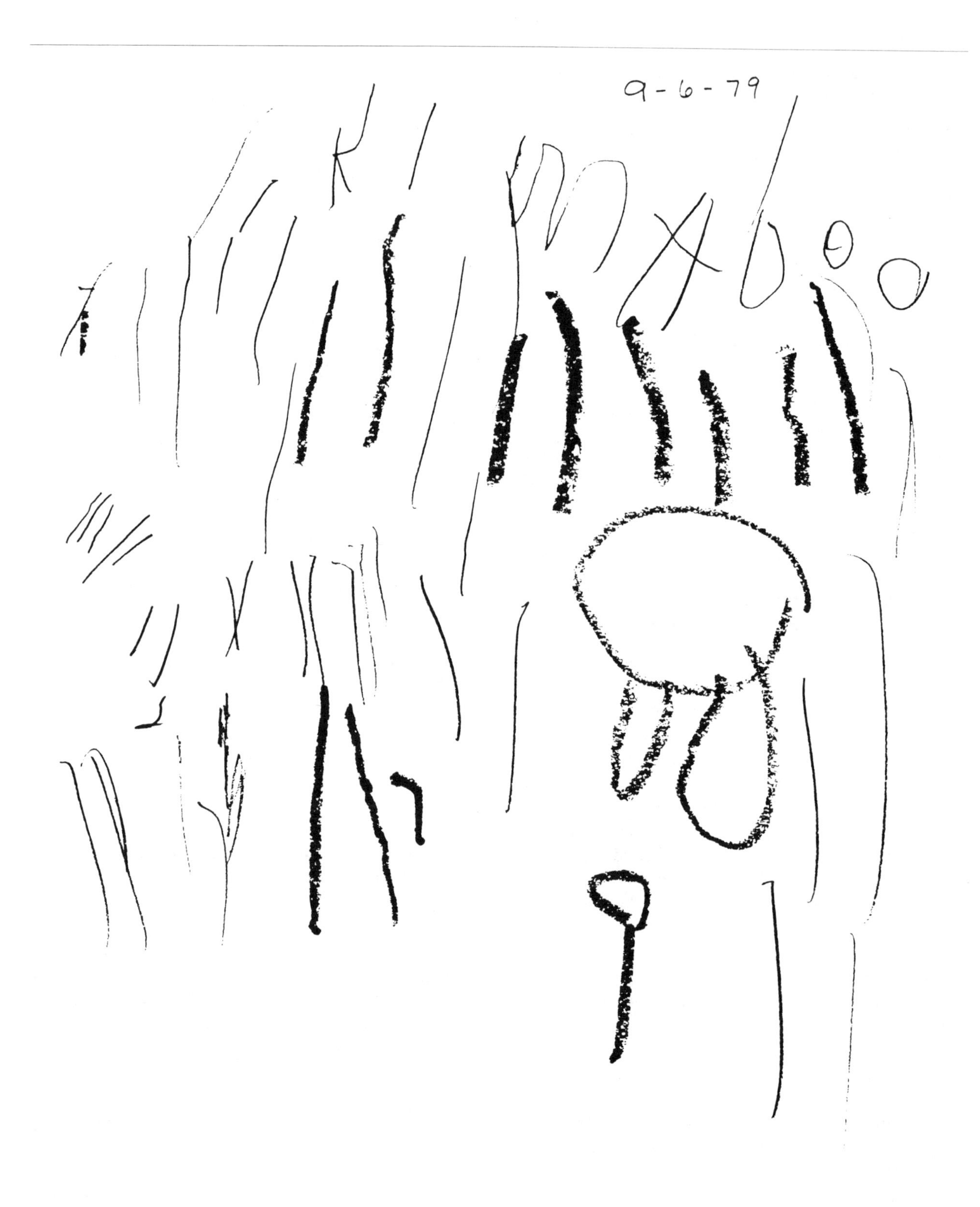

FIGURE 3-12 Front of a Student's Paper During Lesson—Letter / and Art

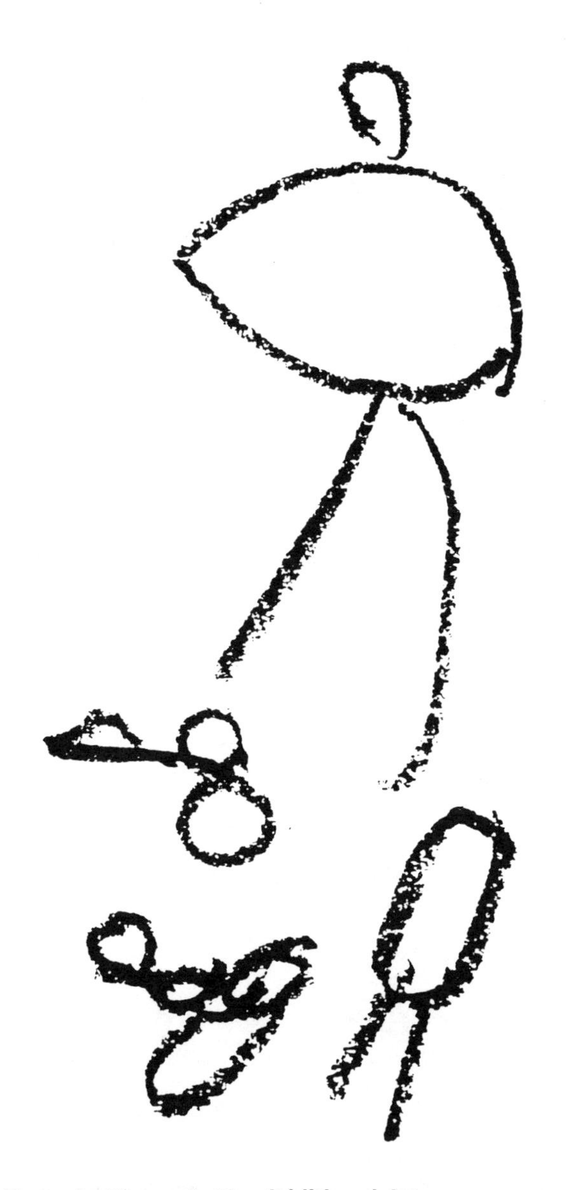

FIGURE 3-13 **Back Side of the Same Paper in Figure 3-12—Additional Art**

FIGURE 3–14 Example of a Kindergarten Student's Coloring in Lesson 2

FIGURE 3-15 Back of the Paper Shown in Figure 3-14—Lesson 2, Letter *t*

FIGURE 3-16 Example of a Student's Art and Writing in Lesson 24, Alphabet Module

FIGURE 3–17 **Example of a Student's Coloring During Lesson 35, Phase II**

FIGURE 3–18 **The Back of the Page Shown in Figure 3–17**

Supply words only if the students cannot think of any. Write some of the words volunteered that do *not* contain the pattern in a space apart from the other words to let the students observe the difference. For example, if the day's module pattern is *fl* (Lesson 58) and a student volunteers *horse*, write *horse* on the chalkboard apart from the words volunteered that contain *fl* to show the students there is no *fl* in the word *horse*. Do not elaborate on the matter. Immediately begin to sound *fl* asking for a word that has *fl* in it. A part of the learning taking place involves which words *do not* as well as *do* have a certain sound pattern in them.

It does not matter if the words containing the pattern are written in a list or scattered on the board. Students are not expected to be able to read the words—they are watching the words being written and hearing the sound(s) of at least one part of the word as it is written.

Since a letter combination does not always have the same sound, use the sounding technique as only one approach, not the end result. If for example, you decided to add the pattern *ap* to the patterns suggested for Phase III, accept any words that contain *ap*, even if the sound of *ap* is not the same in each word:

EXAMPLE: *ap*ply *ap*ple *ap*e

Do not eliminate any words because they might be "too difficult" or because everyone might not know the meaning. If no child knows the meaning, that is reason enough to put it on the board, and naturally talk briefly about its meaning. Vocabulary expansion can take place in this way.

Phase III is a good time to introduce individual students to the *dictionary*. When the pattern is identified, you can show one student the part of the dictionary that has words beginning with that pattern. The student should not be required to read the words; however, he or she may be able to spell the letters and then you can pronounce the word. The next day, a different student might use the dictionary until all have been introduced to it. Usually when you give a hint of the meaning of a word found by a student in the dictionary, the students may recognize it.

You also may need a dictionary. If you are not certain of the spelling of a word volunteered by a student, use the dictionary in front of the class. Students need to see the model of an adult using a dictionary.

3. After two or more words containing the initial pattern are written on the chalkboard or chart paper, each student should have the opportunity to write either letters within a word, some or all of the words on the chalkboard, or any other words containing the pattern. The art element is retained in Phase III. The students might write the words containing the pattern on or beside their artwork, or on the back of the art side of the paper. Each student can draw and make a design of the words or parts of words around a predrawn picture, as a variation.

Refer to Figure 3-19, an example of a student's paper from one of the kindergarten classes during Lesson 57. The initial pattern was *br*, and the student decided to draw a person. Note the words he selected to write around the drawing. No two students wrote the same words on the same place on their papers.

4. Each day, as the last part of this module, each student dates and files his or her paper in the box labeled *Alphabet Module Papers*. If the student has been present each day and completed any writing/art on a paper, there should now be 57 papers in his or her manila folder in the *Alphabet Module Papers* box.

Guidelines for Teaching Phase IV—Final Patterning-Rhyming Words, Lessons 73–100

Beginning with Lesson 73, the emphasis within the Alphabet Modules changes from initial patterns to final patterns, such as rhyming words. Teach this part of the Alphabet Module in the following manner:

1. Write a rhyming starter word on the chalkboard.

EXAMPLE: Lesson 73—red

Ask students for words that rhyme with *red* and write those words on the chalkboard.

EXAMPLES: Zed,
Ned,
bed,
fed

(If a word such as *said* is volunteered, write it on a separate part of the chalkboard and call students' attention to the fact that *said* does not end in the

FIGURE 3-19 Example of a Student's Paper from Lesson 57—*br* Pattern In Words

spelling *ed* although some people pronounce the ending of *said* similarly to the *ed* ending sound.

2. Students begin writing parts or all of these rhyming words on their art papers. Students should feel free to substitute their own words. You should move around the classroom helping students form letters and read the words. Occasionally, you might have students fold their paper, write the words on one side, unfold the paper, and write the words again. Many students actually enjoy doing this.

Refer to Figure 3-20, an example of a student's paper during Lesson 76. The student drew a picture of a *frog* (which was, but did not have to be, the starter word for that day in the Alphabet Module), colored the frog using crayons, and wrote the words *frog, log, hog.* He repeated the words and added one "word" of his own—rog.

Refer to Figure 3-21, an example of a student's paper from one kindergarten class during Lesson 82 in Phase IV. The student wrote words rhyming with *nail.* The teacher, positively reinforcing the student, drew a picture and added rhyming words with a different ending pattern to describe the student's work—Super Duper.

3. At the end of the module, students' papers are dated and filed in their folders. Some teachers prefer to have students write their names and the date on the paper *before* they begin their art/writing activity.

Guidelines for Teaching Phase V—Various Vowels, Lessons 101-120

Although every word volunteered by students or the teacher in the preceding Phases has had at least one vowel in it, the emphasis beginning with Phase V in Lesson 101 is on various vowel spellings and/or sounds. There is no intent to learn vowel rules or to overly categorize words that have a certain vowel spelling, such as *ee* or *oi* in them. The sounds or lack of sounds of vowels within words is also minimized in this Phase. The object is to call the students' attention to various ways vowels are used.

In each module in Phase V, there is a suggested vowel or vowel combination. Lessons 101-110 emphasize long vowel sounds; Lessons 111-120 emphasize other vowel sounds. There should be *at least two* words written on the chalkboard or on chart paper that have particular vowel or vowel combinations. Other words written on the board each day can have any vowels in them. Since vowels in words frequently are overtly illogical, you may need to write the two words on the board.

Do not spend the majority of introductory time in this module searching for several words with a particular vowel spelling. On the other hand, students' attention should be called to different vowel usages. You may do this in your own comfortable, relaxed, and informal way through discussing and pointing to the vowels.

Use the following procedure in teaching the Alphabet Module in Phase V:

1. Write the letters *ee* on the chalkboard or on chart paper taped to the chalkboard.

EXAMPLE: Lesson 101—ee

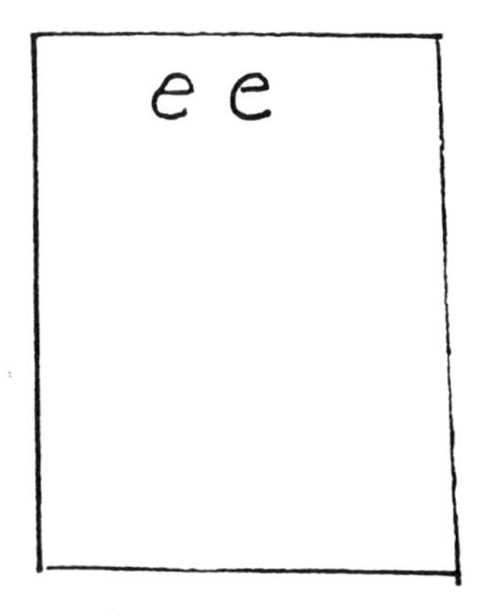

2. Write words volunteered by students that have the *ee* letter cluster spelling and the long *e* sound.

EXAMPLE: flee

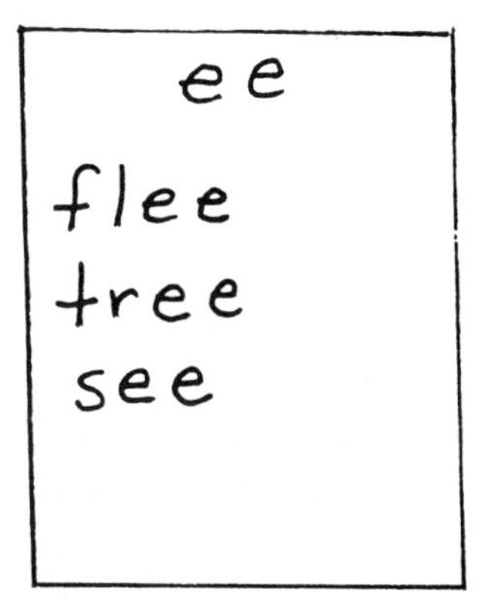

FIGURE 3-20 Example of a Student's Art and Writing from Lesson 76—Rhyming Words Phase

FIGURE 3–21 Example of a Student's Paper from Lesson 82 in Phase IV—Words that Rhyme with *Nail*

If students volunteer words that have the long *e* sound but spellings other than *ee*, write those words on a different section of the chalkboard or the opposite side of the chart paper so students can observe the differences in spelling.

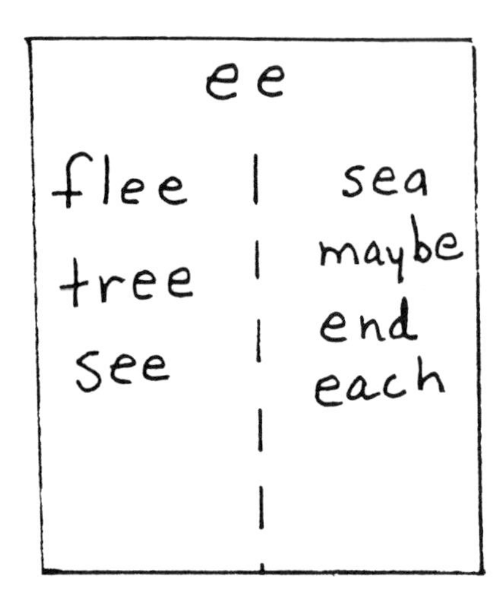

3. Each day, before the end of this module, each student should have time to do an art activity as well as write some of the words or parts of words before dating and filing the paper in the Alphabet Module Papers box.

Students become aware of the various ways vowels are used in words. At this point, *awareness* is the object, not spelling mastery.

One objective of Phase V of the Alphabet Module is auditory training for sound and word building. By selecting one letter cluster, students have a focal point for comparison of sounds and/or spellings. Accept all student responses and use the module symbol(s) as a comparison point in explaining differences. Word meanings should be made informally during the brief discussions about each word.

Beginning with Lesson 111 and continuing through Lesson 120 in Phase V, the major focus is on vowel sounds *other* than long vowels. Teach this part of the Alphabet Module in the following manner:

1. Write the letter *a* on the chalkboard or on chart paper taped to the chalkboard. Write a word volunteered by a student that contains the spelling of *a* but does not have the long *a* sound.

EXAMPLE: Lesson 111—a: Anne

2. Ask students to give as many words as they can that have an *a* in them. Some teachers preferred to make word list groupings. For example, put words volunteered that contain the short *a* sound in one list; words that contain an *a* with a different sound or no sound in a separate list. If students volunteered a word that contained a long *a* sound, that word was put on a section of the chalkboard apart from the other words or lists of words.

EXAMPLE: Lesson 111—a

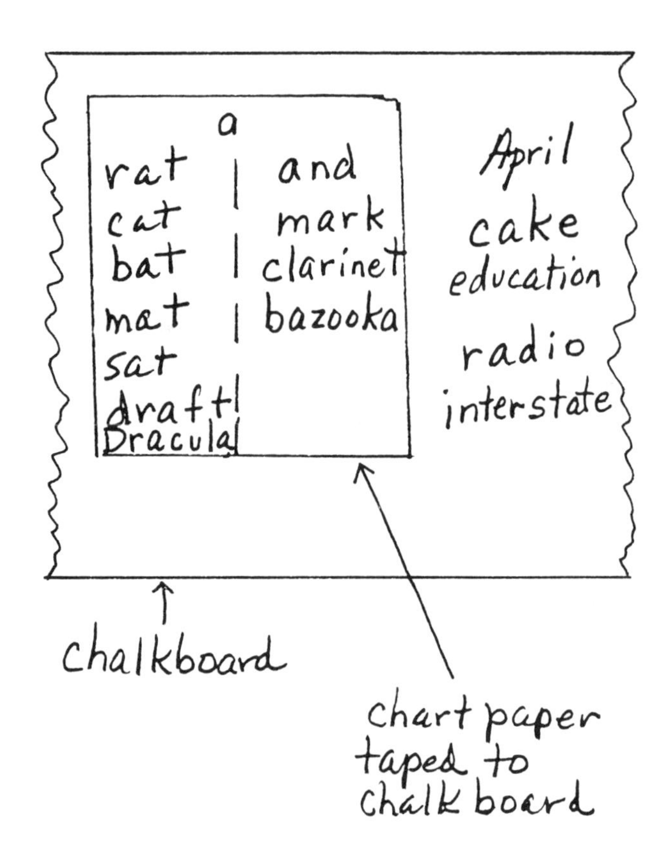

In the drawing the first list of words have the short *a* sound in them (or a sound close to the short *a*)—*rat, draft, mat, Dracula,* etc. The second list on the chart paper contains words volunteered by students that had neither distinct short or long *a* sounds—*mark, bazooka,* etc. A Magic Marker was used to write these words. The third list was written on the chalkboard, and these words have the long *a* sound or a sound close to long *a*—*education, radio, April,* etc. It is not necessary to be scientifically exact in differentiating sounds when working with kindergarten-age children.

3. You rarely have to volunteer words during this part of Phase V. Many students, for example, have the letter *a* in their names, and they may volunteer those as words during Lesson 111. The program has been under way for over 100 days, and most of the students are aware of vowels in words, even though they have never received an emphasis in instruction as found in Phase V. Prior to Phase V, you are referred *informally* to vowels as they were written in words.

Continue to voice the *name* of each consonant and vowel as it is written on the chalkboard or chart paper.

4. Each day before the end of the module, each should write some of the words or some of the letters within a word on a sheet of paper. In addition, there should be an opportunity for each student to illustrate one or more of the words.

You should continue each day to help students create a sentence containing some of the words volunteered and written that day. The sentence is written at the bottom of the chart paper or on the chalkboard. Note the sentence in the illustration below. Words within the sentence should not be restricted; however, each sentence should contain at least *one* word volunteered that day that does not have the long *a* sound. The sentence noted in the illustration was one that was developed in a kindergarten *Success* class during Lesson 111.

a
rat | and | April
cat | mark | cake
bat | clarinet | education
mat | bazooka | radio
sat | | interstate
draft
Dracula

In April, a bat sat on the clarinet.

During the writing of the sentence, the teacher asked the students what kind of letter should begin the sentence, and they replied with enthusiasm "Capital I." The teacher referred to the comma as she put it in the sentence, and the students told the teacher to put a period at the end of the sentence because a question was not asked.

Many of the students wrote sentences rather than single words during the latter part of Lesson 111 and illustrated their sentence by drawing and coloring. Some of the students were using a dictionary. The teacher went from student to student, commenting on something that student had written or wanted to write. *This is the true form of individualized instruction.*

5. All students could write their names, the date, and file the paper in the Alphabet Module Papers box.

Guidelines for Teaching Phase VI—Object Labeling, Lessons 121-130

Beginning with Lesson 121, the focus of the Alphabet Module changes from an emphasis on selecting words containing vowel sounds to selecting and writing words for classroom objects. Traditionally, teachers have made flash cards and taped them to various items in the classroom, such as an *aquarium*, a *desk*, *coat rack*, etc. In Phase VI, with assistance when necessary from the teacher, the *students* make the flash cards and place them on or near the appropriate object.

The alphabet emphasis in Phase VI is on *consonants within whole words.* Teach this part of the module in the following manner:

1. Write the consonants on the chalkboard.

EXAMPLE: Lesson 121—ch and l

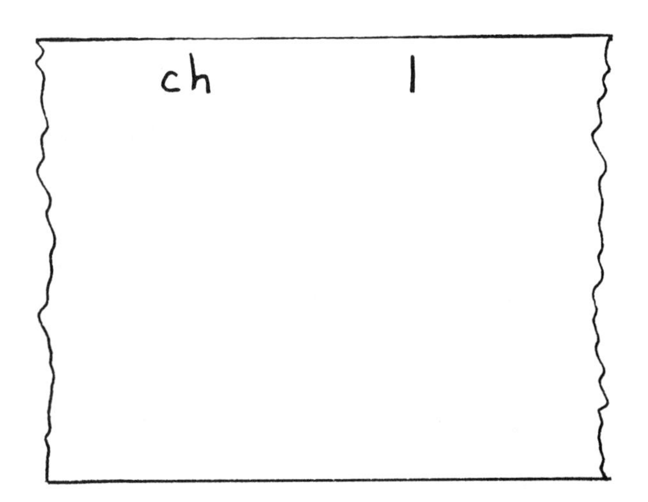

Students volunteer words for objects in the classroom that contain *ch* and/or *l*. As each word is volunteered, write the word on the chalkboard. At least one word for each of the consonant(s) emphasized in that module should be on the board. If students cannot think of a word, you should provide one. Continue to say the name of each letter as it is written. It is not necessary to have a large number of words on the chalkboard.

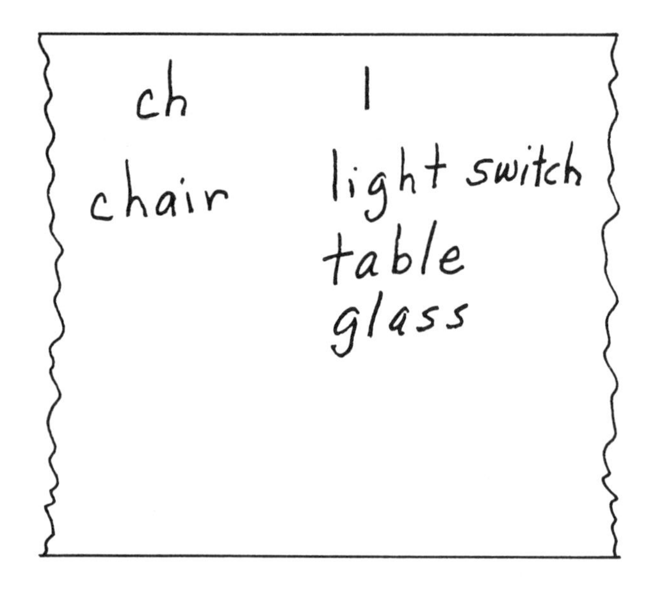

2. Students make their own flash cards, each card containing one of the words on the board or a word not on the board but containing either *ch* or *l*. Many students think of their own words. Although each student should be given the opportunity to try to make one flash card, many students may want to create several cards.

The students place or tape their cards either on the object or near it. There may be 20 cards on the same object, if 20 students write the same word. Students may draw a picture of the object on the flash card. Each student writes his or her name on the flash card.

Figure 3-22 shows examples of flash cards made by students during Lesson 126. The cards were placed around a vase in the classroom. During this same lesson, other students wrote the word *hand* and put their flash cards around a picture of a hand that was on a table. Still other students made flash cards and put them on empty milk cartons in the classroom.

3. The student's name and date should be written on each flash card. The next school day, the flash card made the day before is filed in the student's folder in the Alphabet Module Papers box and the student makes a new flash card or several cards to display in the classroom. Only one card needs to be filed each day in the folder.

Guidelines for Phase VII—Dictation, Lessons 131-154

Beginning with Phase VII in Lesson 131, the emphasis in the Alphabet Module changes from students writing whole words to label objects in the classroom, to students writing words or pasting words on paper that contain certain letters of the alphabet after hearing the words spoken or dictated by the teacher or by another student. The major difference in Phase VII and the preceding phases is the element of the teacher or a student dictating a word, emphasizing each letter sound and voicing letter names as the students write the word. Words selected for use in Phase VII should be those that do not have irregular spellings.

This is an introductory study skill incorporated within Phase VII and is intended to introduce students to the concept of writing words spoken by someone else. Again, mastery is not the goal; however, students enjoy attempting to write words or parts of words they hear.

There is a mixture of single consonants (*l* in Lesson 131) and consonant clusters (*sp* in Lesson 134) in Phase VII. Teach Phase VII in the following manner:

1. You or the student pronounces a designated sound, a word containing the letter sound, and *slowly* pronounces the letter sounds within the word. Do not pronounce the letter name.

> *EXAMPLE:* Lesson 131—*l: leg* (the sound of *l-e-g)*

Students write the letters for the sounds they hear.

Figure 3-23 is an example of one student's paper developed during Lesson 151. The emphasis is on the letter cluster *st* so the student cut out words containing *st* from a magazine and pasted them on paper. Students can work in pairs during Phase VII if you so direct.

2. Each student's paper is dated and filed in the Alphabet Module Papers box.

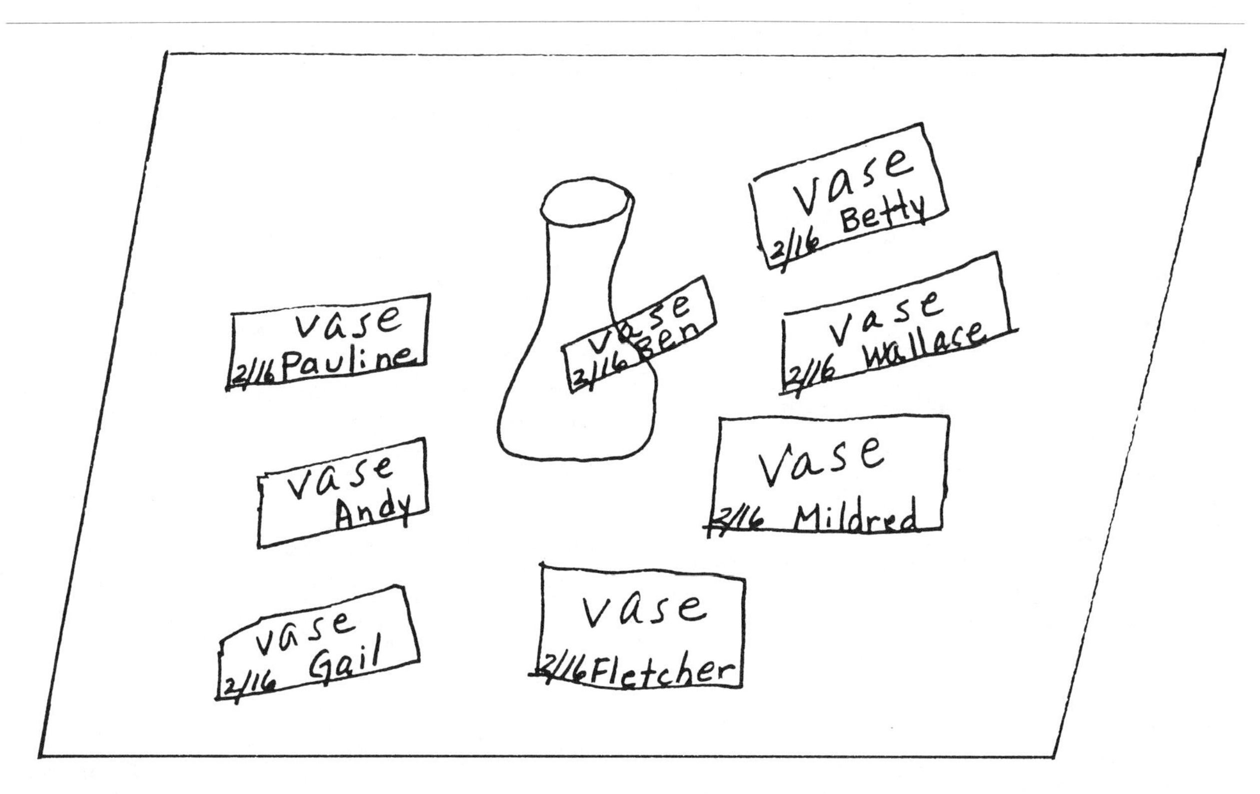

FIGURE 3–22 Example of Object Labeling from Lesson 26

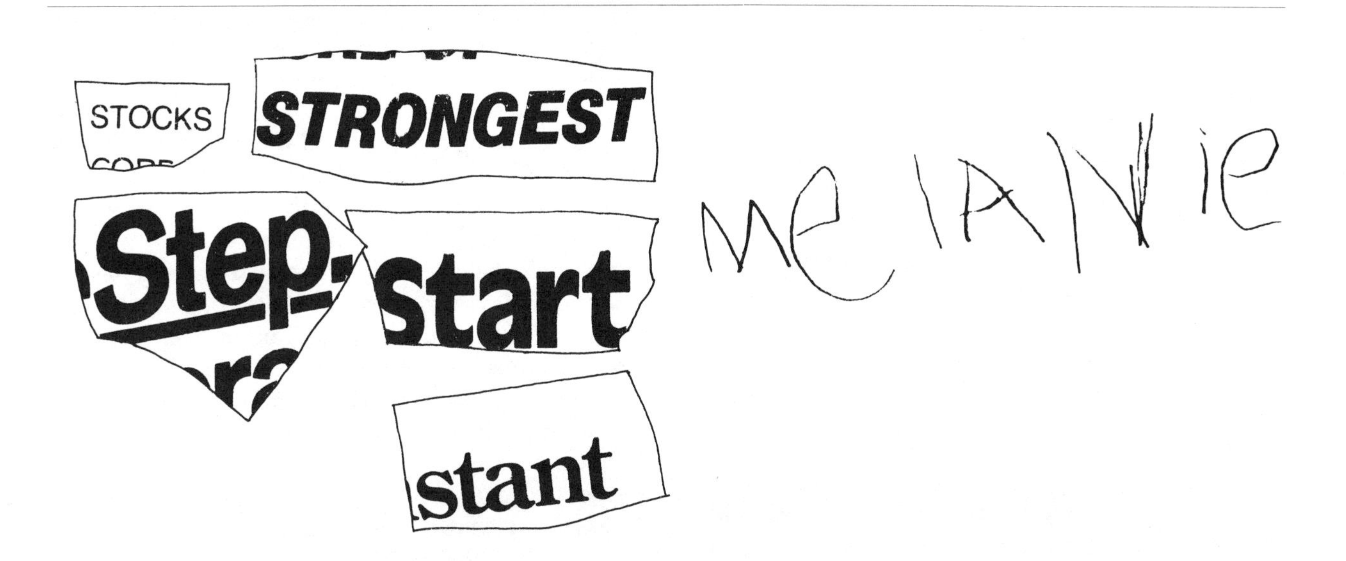

FIGURE 3–23 Example of a Student's Paper from Lesson 151—Words Containing *ST*

Guidelines for Teaching Phase VIII—Completion, Lessons 155-180

The last Phase, Consonant Completion, places the emphasis on the student selecting initial letters when supplied with the remainder of the word. Some students can put these words in sentences and stories of their own writing; others will like to write the words only; a very few students may still be learning how to write single letters. As in the other Phases, all students are not asked to write the same things; however, you should help each student to write something successfully, whether a story or a part of a letter.

Phase VIII balances and reinforces the earlier Rhyming Words emphasis in Phase IV. Teach Phase VIII in the following manner:

1. Write on the chalkboard all of the letters in a word *with the exception of the initial consonant(s).* Lessons 155–180 in Appendix One have suggestions for words. Discuss words that can be made by adding different consonants. Do not write the consonants on the chalkboard. Students write on paper at their desks different words containing the same ending and a different initial consonant or consonant cluster.

EXAMPLE: Lesson 60:

___at
bat
hat
fat
format

You should help each student to experience some degree of success in this Phase, whether he or she is still at the letter formation stage or is writing several of these words in sentences or stories.

Figure 3-24 is an example of one student's paper developed during Lesson 164. The consonant completion emphasis is on the letters before *one* at the ending of words, and of course, the *n* in *one.* Students wrote initial letters to form different words ending with the *one* spelling.

2. Each student each day dates and files his or her paper in the *Alphabet Module Papers* box. Most of the students complete art work on the paper before filing it.

SUMMARY OF PHASES IMPACT

Although each of the eight Phases has a distinct focus, there is an opportunity for overlap and reinforcement among the Phases. For example, vowels, rhyming words, and dictation can be emphasized at any point within any module. With the *Success* plan, there is a base structure that does not keep students in the same mold nor try to handicap their unique individuality; yet, is designed to help them move forward. The following is a summary of the educational focus of each Phase:

In Phases I and II (Lessons 1-52), students receive special professional assistance in learning to form lower and upper case letters of the alphabet, although these Phases are not limited only to letter formation.

During Phase III (Lessons 53-72), the emphasis is on providing opportunities for students (1) to volunteer words that *begin with the same alphabet letters,* (2) to observe the writing of some of these words, and (3) to write some of the words themselves.

During Phase IV (Lessons 73-100), the emphasis is on providing opportunities for students (1) to develop a listening sense for rhyming words, and (2) to observe the writing of the words that have the same final alphabet letters. To balance the focus of Phase III on word beginnings, Phase IV emphasizes word endings.

During Phase V (Lessons 101-120), the emphasis is on words that contain the *sound* of a vowel—*a, e, i, o,* or *u.* In a few instances, the vowel may not be in the word, as for example, *eight* has the long *a* sound and yet contains the vowels *e* and *i.* The word *eight* would be recorded as a word containing the long *a* sound. You should briefly call attention to the unique spelling of these kinds of words. Words containing both uncluttered spelling of vowels and the long sound of that vowel will not need such special considerations. During Phase V the emphasis is also on words containing at least one vowel and *any vowel sound(s)* other than the long vowel sounds.

During Phase VI (Lessons 121-130), the emphasis is on locating objects in the classroom that contain a designated alphabet letter. The *students* make their own word flash cards and place them as labels on or near the appropriate objects.

During Phase VII (Lessons 131-154), the emphasis is on you dictating a letter or letter cluster and students locating words *from a variety of printed sources* that contain the letter(s). They might write the words or parts of the words found in books or other nonconsumable materials, and/or remove words from newspapers and other con-

FIGURE 3-24 Example of a Student's Paper Developed During Lesson 164—Consonant Completion Emphasis on the *N* in *One*

TABLE 3-2 Letter Patterns

Lessons	Patterns
1-26	Lower case single alphabet letters
27-52	Upper case single alphabet letters
53-72	Two-letter patterns beginning with *gr, sp, fr, bl, br, fl, pl, sl, sh, sm, tr, wh, th, cl, sk, st, sw, spl, spr, thr*
73-100	Words that rhyme with *red, drill, cup, frog, charm, pain, grind, blame, car, nail, mop, rake, close, leaf, dime, brain, table, same, fog, light, growl, slow, toaster, Jack, Nell, spring, cow, sit*
101-110	Vowels—long sounds in words that contain *ee, a, i, o, u, o_e, igh, y, oa, ow*
111-120	Vowel sounds other than long vowel sounds in words that contain *a, u, i, o, oo, ow, or, aw, ur*
121-130	Object labeling of words containing *ch, l, d, w, b, fl, p, c, q, y, h, m, v, n, r, st, t, f, j, k*
131-154	Alphabet letter dictation of words containing *l, g, wh, sp, m, str, ch, f, r, k* or *e, s, d, t, p, b, h, m, w, th, j, n, fl, qu*
155-180	Consonant completion of words ending with *_ake, _ine, _eed, _are, _een, _at, _ow, _oon, _oke, _one, _ale, _ile, _ool, _ean, _ute, _eel, _um, _ing, _ed, _ir, _oy, _ore, _ule, _ail, _ack, _ight*

sumable materials and paste them on paper. Each day during the Alphabet Module, individual discussions of word meanings should be held between you and the students.

During Phase VIII (Lessons 155–180), the emphasis is on student selection of consonants to complete words. The object is not to select words that can be completed with only one consonant, but rather to teach students that some words can be changed only by changing one letter. (Example: *b*ake, *r*ake, *l*ake, *t*ake). As in all other Phases in the Alphabet Module, the *students* rather than the teacher, volunteer the majority of the words.

Each day in each Phase, students should have opportunities to correlate their art with the writing. Each day, also, their paper is dated and filed.

LETTER PATTERNS

Table 3-2 is a list of the letter patterns suggested in the Alphabet Module in Appendix One. The object is not for the students to memorize the letter combinations or to use them in drill exercises, but rather to observe them in natural settings throughout the year.

Students who cannot form a letter at the beginning of the school year may be writing words in sentences by the end of the year. Teamed with the Alphabet Module and the other three modules in the *Success* program, you can give the students that opportunity.

chapter four

How to Teach the Oral Language/Reading Module

One purpose of the Oral Language/Reading Module is to correlate a student's spoken vocabulary or dialogue with observation of writing and reading of words.

There is no scheduled block of time for the Oral Language/Reading Module. Instead, during the day, you should teach that day's module theme to as many individuals as you can. For example, one student might be taught the module as he or she approaches your desk first thing in the morning; another student, when he or she is finishing putting a puzzle together; and another during free center time.

Although there is no grouping in this module, some teachers prefer to form small groups to teach the themes. If you form such groups, they should not be on any basis of ability, and group members should change frequently rather than remain constant. While you are teaching the module to one group of students, other students should be engaged in different activities in the classroom.

The theme for each Oral Language/Reading Module is found in the *fourth column* of each lesson in Appendix One. Each module contains a suggested topic for initial conversation; however, you should change the module's suggested theme if it is not appropriate for a particular day, for example if something happens that indicates a theme of greater immediate interest to the students. Children enjoy talking about *chewing bubble gum*, *playing king and queen*, and *jumping in mud puddles.* These kinds of items are included in the Oral Language/Reading Module of the *Success* program. In addition, traditional kinds of kindergarten class topics, such as *sharing*, *safety*, and *holidays are included as themes.*

This module incorporates individual student's language and provides opportunities for each student to observe some of his or her words written by the teacher, a parent, an aide, or another volunteer in the classroom.

HOW TO TEACH THE ORAL LANGUAGE/READING MODULE

It may not be possible to teach the module to every student every day; however, hopefully, each student will receive the module once every two days. For this reason, each theme is continued for two days for the first 80 lessons of this module. At the beginning of the year, the module takes less than two minutes to teach to a student—time for you to write one word spoken by the student and the student's name. Later, you may write additional words spoken by the student, and the student writes his or her name. Words written are always displayed *by the student*, not by you.

There are three basic procedures in teaching the Oral Language/Reading Module:

1. Discuss *briefly* with one student a particular theme (see Appendix One, Oral Language/Reading Module).

2. Write with a Magic Marker *at least one word* spoken by the student and the student's name on a small strip of construction paper.

3. The student tacks or tapes the construction paper strip on a bulletin board on some small space designated as that student's display spot in the classroom.

THE PHASES THROUGHOUT THE ACADEMIC YEAR

The sequence in the fourth column in Appendix One is developmental, intended to move from the teacher doing the writing, to stages in which some students make their own displays or words and sentences. On the other hand, all students are not required nor expected to move at the same rate.

There are three Phases in the Oral Language/Reading Module. Each Phase incorporates the emphases of the preceding Phases and extends the concepts to include new dimensions.

Table 4-1 is an overview of the Phases, lessons, and Phase emphases:

The basic sequence is from single words to more than one word (word clusters) to use of a word cluster in a sentence.

Guidelines for Teaching Phase I—Single Words Spoken by a Student, Lessons 1-80

You, another adult, or students should cut strips of construction paper prior to the first day of the *Success* program. Strips used for Phase I need to be large enough only to accommodate the writing of one word and a student's first name. Figure 4-1 is an example of two student responses to the theme *pretty things* in Lesson 8 and *school* in Lesson 9. During Phases II and III, the strips need to be longer to afford room to write several words and sentences.

1. Note the theme in the fourth column in Appendix One. For example, the theme for Lesson 1 is *toys*. Ask one student to mention one toy he or she likes. If the student responds, "*I like super trucks*," write only the word *trucks* on the strip of construction paper and that student's name. Early in the year, it is more important to have at least one word written as spoken by as many students as possible than to have several words spoken by a fewer number of students.

trucks
Ellen

Both you and the student name the letters within the word *as you write it*. Therefore, it is imperative for the student to observe the writing of his or her word. You can note the various sounds of letter(s) within the word being written.

2. Show the students how to use a thumb tack or masking tape to display the strip of paper in the classroom. Once the student knows how to do this, he or she can do it independently, allowing you time to write a word for another student.

Do not ask students to "wait their turn" for this module. It is best if it is taught informally. Simply work with a student as the opportunity allows. Soon they will learn the procedure, want their word displayed, and let you know if they have not had an opportunity that day.

TABLE 4-1

Phase	Emphasis	Lessons
I	Single word spoken by student	1-80
II	Picture/word cluster associations	81-100
III	Sentences containing a specific word cluster	101-180

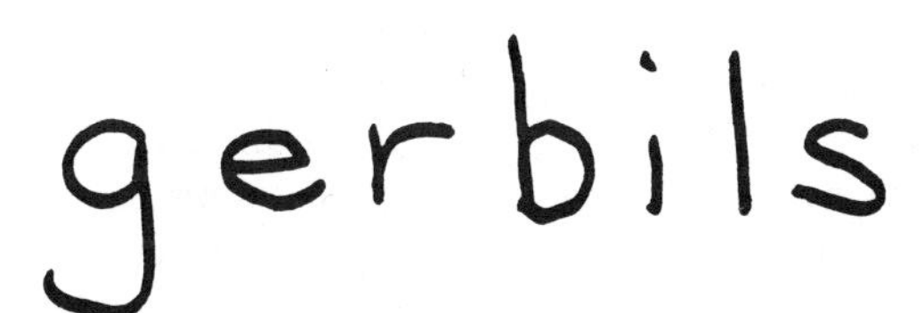

FIGURE 4-1 **Example of Two Different Student Responses to Lessons 8 and 9 of the Oral Language/Reading Module**

Students who can write their own names on the first day of kindergarten should be given the chance to do so. As students learn to write during the year, encourage them to write their own words on the strips of paper.

Some small section of the classroom would be ideal for each student to claim as his or her own display area—a part of a bulletin board, a part of a flannel board, a side of a desk, or a part of the door. After each student places his or her recorded conversation strip on a bulletin board or some other area of the classroom, the strip remains there until the student has had an opportunity to participate in more Oral Language/Reading Modules. The student puts the new strip on the bulletin board and takes the old home.

Puppets are excellent for encouraging reluctant children to talk during this module. The puppets become intermediaries for conversations. The puppets do not need to be expensive; they can be made from small paper bags or socks. Using puppets is left to the discretion of the individual teacher. Some kindergarten teachers thoroughly enjoyed using puppets, while others preferred not to use them.

Holding a puppet, a student is encouraged to enter the discussion with another puppet you are holding. Record on a strip of construction paper words "spoken" by the puppet/student.

The conversation during the Oral Language/Reading Module should be guided so the theme of the writing relates to at least one recognizable topic, which may be the theme suggested in the lesson. For example, in Figure 4-1, a *pretty thing* to Melanie was a *gerbil* in Lesson 8; Claudia associates *playing* with *school* in Lesson 9. It is important to include a variety of themes during this module.

Figure 4-2 contains an example of the kind of words that students might volunteer for the Oral Reading/Language Module in Lesson 15 and 16 where the discussion theme was *shopping*. Note the variety of topics, the repetition of *toys*, and the inclusion of unexpected items, such as *ice*. Note that the words were recorded on two different days.

Guidelines for Teaching Phase II—Picture/Word Cluster Associations, Lessons 81-100

Beginning with Phase II, the strips of paper should be longer so you or the student can write more than one word. In Phase I, some strips contained word clusters; however, the emphasis was on having at least one word on the strip. In Phase II, the emphasis is on having more than one word (word cluster) on the strip of paper.

Use the same teaching procedure as suggested for Phase I of the Oral Language/Reading Module. Since some of the students can now write, the discussion theme is changed each day to afford a greater variety of knowledge area topics.

A variation introduced in Phase II is the use of magazines or other small pictures. Each day during Phase II, instead of writing on construction paper strips, the student might locate a picture he or she can associate with the module theme. At least one cluster of words spoken by the student and the student's name are written on or near the picure. The picture may be glued on newsprint or some other paper and the words written on the paper so they will be visible. The student then displays the picture in the classroom.

Continue to write for those students who cannot do so, and make content or spelling suggestions for those students who can write. Every word spoken by a student does not need to be recorded.

Figure 4-3 contains examples of word clusters students might volunteer during Lesson 96 where the discussion topic is *inside a refrigerator*.

Guidelines for Teaching Phase III—Sentences Containing Specific Word Clusters, Lessons 101-180

Although sentences may have been written on some of the construction paper strips or magazine pictures in Phases I and II, the emphasis of oral communication/writing in Phase III is on helping each student speak a sentence and observing the writing of that sentence. Additional time is required for the sentence writing; therefore, module themes are repeated for two consecutive days. Hopefully, each student will be taught this module at least once every two days.

In the Oral Language/Reading Module there is a suggested word cluster that can be used as a reference point. For example, in Lesson 163, the cluster is *watching a game*. You might say to a student, "What do you see when you watch a game?" If the student replies, "I see people win," you might write the sentence, "Billy sees people win." on a strip of construction paper. The exact word cluster suggested for each module in Lessons 101-180 does *not* need to be included in the written sentences. Phase III can also be correlated with art, if the stu-

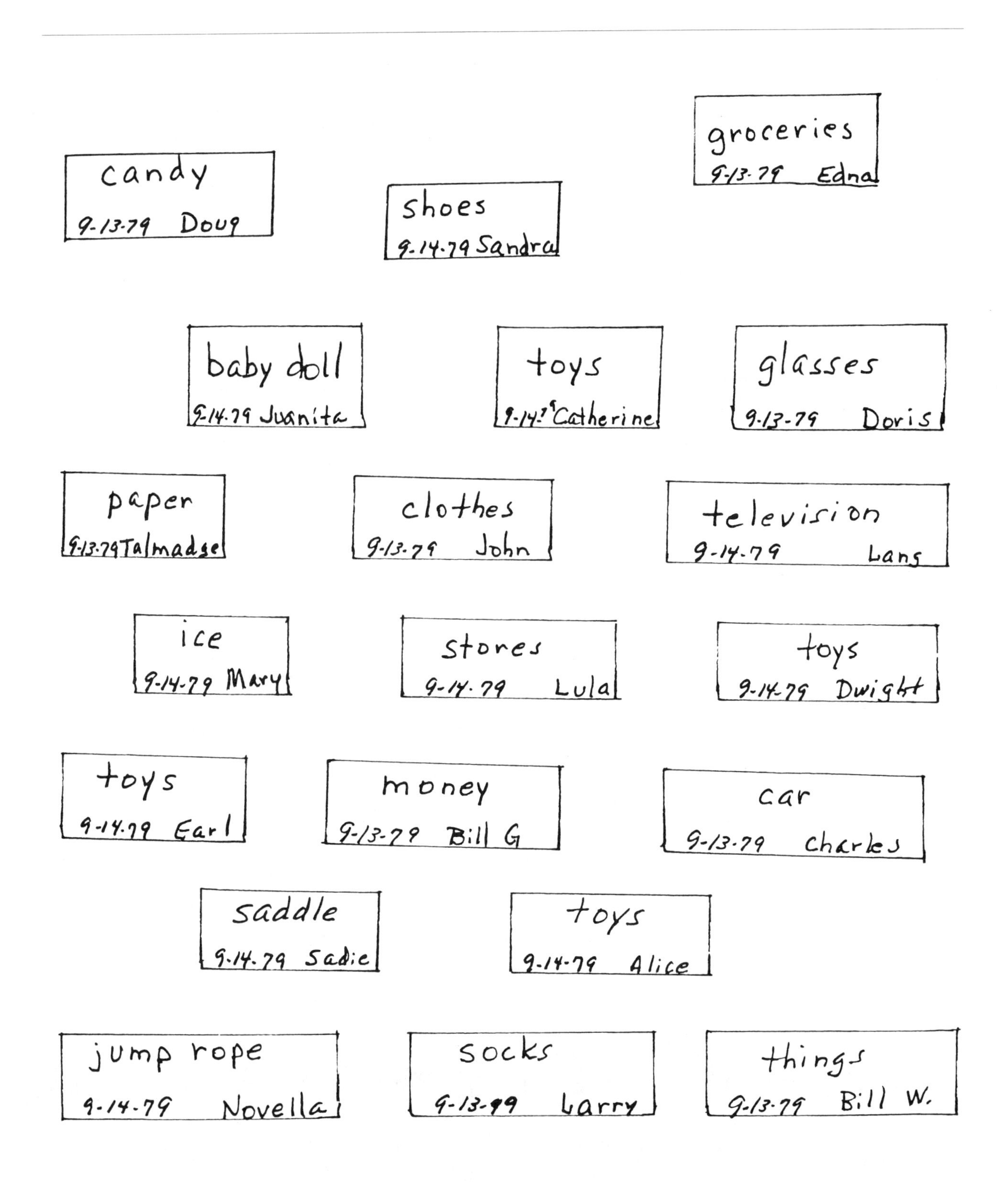

FIGURE 4-2 **Phase I Examples of Words Volunteered by Students in Lessons 15–16**

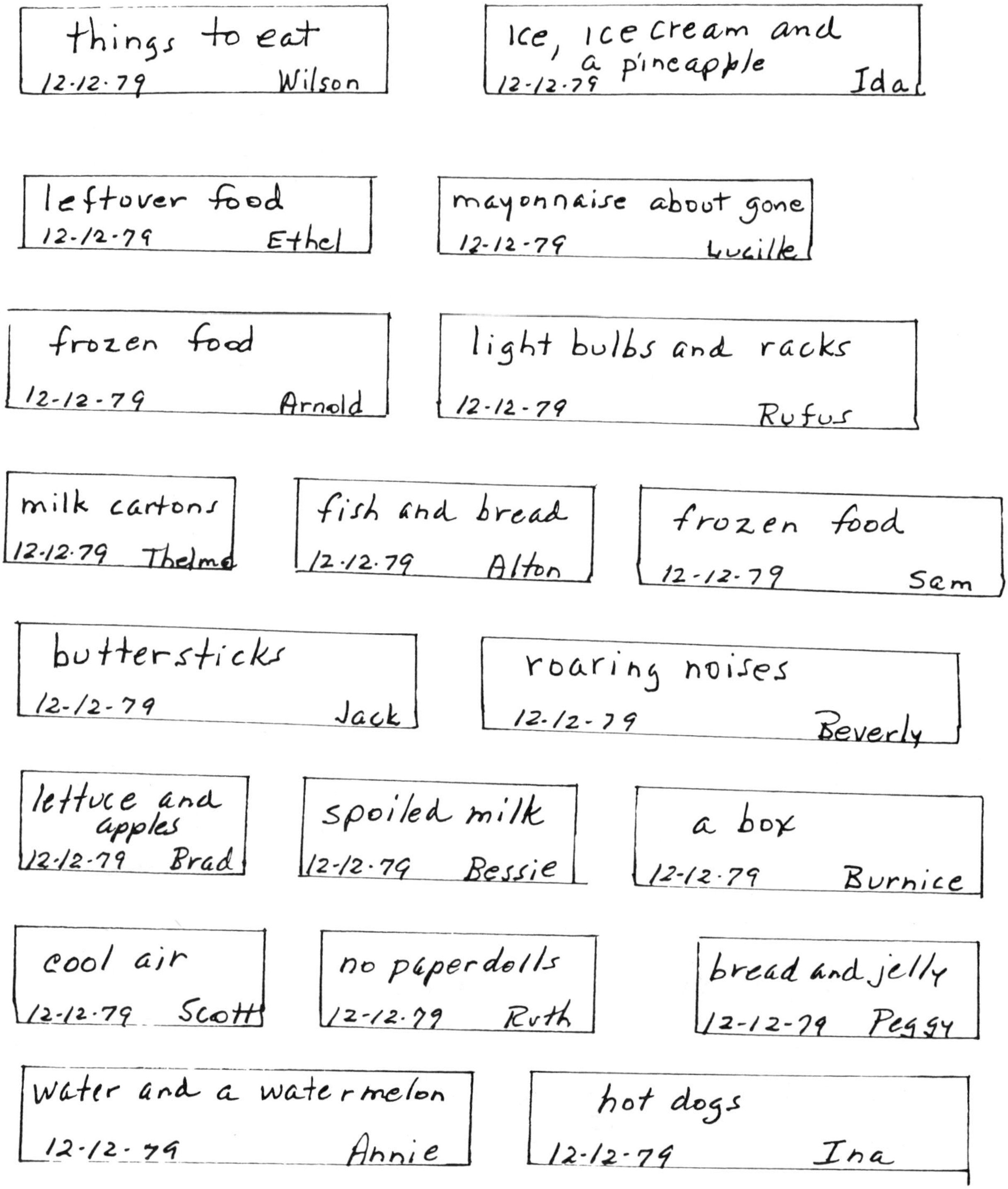

things to eat
12-12-79 Wilson

Ice, ice cream and a pineapple
12-12-79 Ida

leftover food
12-12-79 Ethel

mayonnaise about gone
12-12-79 Lucille

frozen food
12-12-79 Arnold

light bulbs and racks
12-12-79 Rufus

milk cartons
12-12-79 Thelma

fish and bread
12-12-79 Alton

frozen food
12-12-79 Sam

buttersticks
12-12-79 Jack

roaring noises
12-12-79 Beverly

lettuce and apples
12-12-79 Brad

spoiled milk
12-12-79 Bessie

a box
12-12-79 Burnice

cool air
12-12-79 Scott

no paperdolls
12-12-79 Ruth

bread and jelly
12-12-79 Peggy

water and a watermelon
12-12-79 Annie

hot dogs
12-12-79 Ina

FIGURE 4-3 Phase II Examples of Words Volunteered by Students in Lesson 96

dent draws a picture on the strip to illustrate his or her sentence.

Use the same teaching procedure for Phase III of the Oral Language/Reading Module as used in Phases I and II. The module topic is the noun in each discussion theme in Lessons 101–180. For example, the theme suggested in Lesson 123 is *eating candy*. Thus, the module topic is *candy*.

Whereas early in the year a single word was displayed by each student, in Phase III a sentence is displayed. Students should be able to write letters, letter parts, words, word parts, or complete sentences on their strips of paper with some assistance from the teacher.

Figure 4-4 is an example of sentences that students might volunteer during Phase III, Lessons 143 and 144 where the discussion theme is *eating an ice cream cone.*

SUMMARY OF PHASES

The following is an overview of the three Phases in the Oral Language/Reading Module:

Phase I (Lessons 1–80), emphasizes students observing single words written which they spoke during conversations. These words are displayed in the classroom. Puppets are useful in encouraging students to talk about a particular theme.

Phase II (Lessons 81–100), emphasizes students observing the writing of word clusters they spoke during conversations. These word clusters are displayed in the classroom. Phase II adds the element of *picture content* to expedite discussions.

Phase III (Lessons 101–180), emphasizes sentences students spoke that are recorded by them or the teacher. With some students, the sentences may develop into paragraphs.

There is a strong degree of flexibility among the Phases. For example, although the emphasis in Phase II is on word clusters, some of the content may be in single word or sentence form. In Phase III where the emphasis is on sentences, word clusters may be written. In Phase II the idea is to have each student speak at least one word cluster related to the theme. In Phase III each student speaks at least one sentence related to the theme and records it.

If the students make drawings in connection with the Oral Language/Reading Module, the theme of the drawing should relate to the module's discussion theme.

SELECTED SUBTHEMES

Table 4-2 is a list of selected subtheme areas to include in conversations prior to and during the writing of the words. This list is helpful in parent-teacher conferences in indicating some of the topical areas students will encounter in their kindergarten class if the *Success* topics are used. The list is also helpful to teachers in planning additional topics to include during the year.

The Oral Language/Reading Module compensates for the fact that most people encounter words already written, printed, or written in a sequence suggested by others. Rather than seeing words already in print, every student in this module observes his or her oral contribution, or parts of it, transformed into written language. This process is extremely important. Do not skip this module. The students thoroughly enjoy their words and names displayed in the classroom throughout the year. Students who are reluctant to talk at the beginning of the school year may be recording their own sentences spoken to someone else by the end of the same year.

Everyone wants to eat strawberry ice cream, not vanilla.
3-26-80
Tom

Ice cream is a good thing to eat every day.
3-26-80
Laura

My mother likes ice cream.
3-26-80
Keva

I eat every kind of ice cream, almost.
3-27-80
Virginia

I like ice cream until it melts.
3-27-80
Gerald

Ice cream is good when it is cold.
3-27-80
Kim

Eating ice cream is good
3-27-80
J.P.

Ice cream can hurt as it goes down.
3-27-80
Eugene

FIGURE 4-4 Phase III Examples of Sentences Volunteered by Students During Lessons 143 and 144

TABLE 4–2 Selected Discussion Areas in the Oral Language/Reading Module

pretty things	noisy things	items on a table
giant things	things that move	items inside a refrigerator
things that hurt	hot things	desserts
tiny things	blue things	shopping
smooth things	bouncing things	older people
scary things	living things	younger people
exciting things	green things	growing up
funny things	any two items	persons
groups of things	any three items	getting ready for school
places	happiness	eating lunch
airplanes	sadness	blowing up a balloon
automobiles	licking a lollipop	helping at home
trucks	dancing to music	listening to a story
music	visiting a friend	watching a storm
safety	riding in a car	taking a ride
toys	tying shoe laces	watching a game
playing	reading a book	getting my hair cut
animals	eating candy	eating a snack
food	talking with a teacher	finding a secret place
school	playing with friends	getting presents
time	painting a picture	waving good-bye
friendship	looking at the moon	jumping over a puddle
sharing	watching a TV program	
responsibility	sitting in a chair	
working	building a block castle	
holidays	stringing beads	
birthday	taking a trip	
success	eating an ice cream cone	
love	playing hide and seek	
energy	jumping with a jump rope	
feelings	jumping in the air	
silence	getting shoes	
gentleness	bouncing a ball	
rainy days	combing my hair	
dentist	brushing my teeth	

chapter five

How to Teach the Story Time Module

When interviewing kindergarten teachers as one part of the research in the development of the *Success* program, they agreed unanimously that kindergartners should have stories read to them each day—there was no doubt about that matter.

The *Success* kindergarten program incorporates the traditional reading of stories to students, and adds only one dimension—selecting categories of words for students to see, but not necessarily to read.

The major purpose of the Story Time Module is to provide listening experiences with a *large* number of different books. In addition, you should write on the chalkboard or on chart paper some of the words in the story.

The Story Time Module is the fourth module of a lesson and it lasts for approximately 20 minutes each day.

Categorical suggestions for locating words in the stories are found in the fifth column of each lesson in Appendix One. The major purpose of the categories is to provide a variety of words to emphasize during the year.

HOW TO TEACH THE STORY TIME MODULE

1. Select a library book and write words from the story on the chalkboard or on chart paper. As noted earlier, to avoid undue repetition of the same categories of words, such as *names of characters*, and to expand the kinds of words students hear, there is a suggested word category in each Story Time Module. Refer to the category, skim through the selected story, and write some of the words associated with that category on the chalkboard. Write the words either before or after the story is read, depending on which Phase of the year is under way. (See the next section in this chapter on Phases.)

2. Students form a group near you and you should sit or stand near the words on the chalkboard. Use traditional ways of reading the story to students—mention the title, use appropriate vocal intonations, occasionally turn the book for students to see the pictures (or the colors in the picture if students are far from the book), etc. Read an entire story or part of a longer story to the class each day.

Occasionally, as one of the words or word clusters written on the chalkboard or chart paper is read from the book, use a ruler or yardstick to point to the word(s) and show the student how it looks when written.

3. When the story is finished, optional activities are playing games with the words written on the chalkboard or chart paper, discussing the story, asking students what else could have happened in the story, etc.

Figure 5-1 is an example of words written by one kindergarten teacher for Lessons 5, 11, 22, and 90 in the Story Time Module.

Lesson 5—Word Category: adjectives

country

musical

magic city

Lesson 11—Word Category: character names

Peter Pan Wendy

Tinkerbell

Captain Hook

Lesson 22—Word Category: things that are heard

cat bees

squirrel car

Lesson 90—Word Category: adjectives

big warm wet

tall

FIGURE 5-1 **Examples of Words Written by the Teacher for the Categories for Lessons 5, 11, 22, and 90 in the Story Time Module**

Probably no two teachers will select the same words, even if they read the same story. The following is an example of words selected for Lesson 1 of the Story Time Module where the category of words is *names* and the story read is *Cinderella.*

EXAMPLE: Story—Cinderella

Word category:—names in the story

Cinderella
prince
stepmother
sister
fairy godmother

In this example the story was not finished that day and was continued on the next day. The category of words for Lesson 2 is *places.* The teacher scans the remainder of the story and writes the following words on the chalkboard:

kitchen
house
palace
ballroom

The teacher then points to those words at least once when they appear in the remainder of the story. *Do not require each student to "read" the words on the chalkboard or chart paper.*

When the story is finished, or the module time is over, some teachers provide follow-up or review activities for the students. For example, if words have been written on the chalkboard, a student might "wash the board" by telling a part of the story related to some of the words. A student comes to the board, points to a word(s), and after relating the word(s) with the story, erases the word(s). Another teacher might use the words for review of the Alphabet Module emphasis for that day. Students count letters in the words they have encountered in previous lessons of the Alphabet Module, thus correlating the Story Time Module with mathematics and the alphabet.

Kindergarten teachers who wrote some of the words in the story related to a specific category on chart paper, indicated the lesson number and the word category on the charts so they could be used the following year. For example:

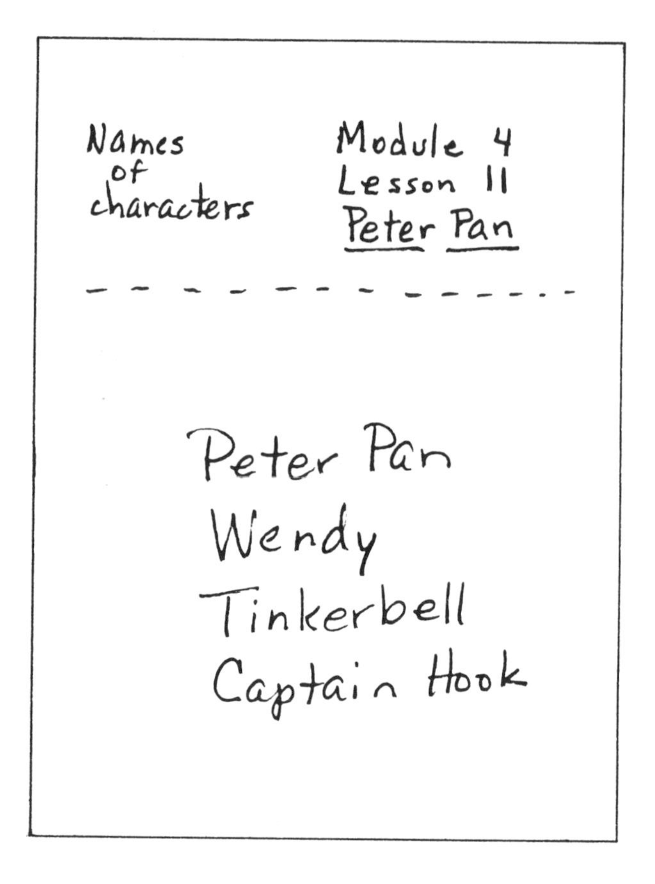

THE PHASES THROUGHOUT THE ACADEMIC YEAR

There are two Phases in the Story Time Module. Each module (Lessons 1–180) contains a category of words that can be found in most fiction.

In Phase I (Lessons 1–100), select some words from the story related to the suggested category and write those words on the chalkboard or chart paper *before* reading the story to the students.

In Phase II (Lessons 101–180), depending on the suggested category in each module, the words are written *before or after* reading the story. For example, you can locate some words associated with *time* in the story (Lesson 125) and write some of those words on the chalkboard before reading the story to the class. On the other hand, writing words or word clusters associated with *main characters* in the story (Lesson 161) might best be accomplished through class discussion after the story is read.

The students receive an additional bonus in both Phases I and II—*seeing* some of the words they *hear* from the story.

Guidelines for Teaching Phase I—Words Written Before the Story is Read, Lessons 1-100

1. Prior to reading a story, refer to the word category area of the Story Time Module in the particular lesson. For example, the category in Lesson 5 is *adjectives* and in Lesson 16 it is *objects.* If Lesson 5 is being taught, scan the book you want to read and write on the chalkboard or chart paper *a few* of the adjectives found in the story, such as *big, green, wonderful.* If Lesson 16 is being taught, scan the book for names of objects in the story, such as *house, box,* or *staples.* Write only a few of the words from the designated category on the chalkboard.

2. Sit or stand, depending on your preference, near the words on the chalkboard or chart paper. As you read the story, use a ruler or yardstick to point to the words *at least once* as each is encountered in the story. It is not necessary to point to each word each time it is read.

Guidelines for Teaching Phase II—Words Written Before or After the Story is Read, Lessons 101-180

Use the same procedure as in Phase I, except you may write the words after you read the story. During Phase II, allow some students to write the words. Follow the suggested categories of words for the Story Time Module to afford a variety of words to write.

SELECTED CATEGORIES OF WORDS

Each day the word category changes in the Story Time Module. It is extremely important to offer a variety of word categories over the academic year, rather than selecting only limited kinds of words.

Table 5-1 is a list of some of the emphasis areas found in the Story Time Module. The list is useful in explaining the module during parent-teacher conferences. You may wish to add other word categories or substitute some categories found in the module. The four major categories are: specific words, descriptive words, parts of speech, and words denoting sequence.

BOOKS IN THE KINDERGARTEN

Selecting the books to use in the Story Time Module is left to your discretion. Frequent input from students in that particular classroom is helpful. The selection will depend to a large extent on the titles of books in the school library.

One of the pilot kindergarten teachers kept a record of the books she read to her class for each day of the year. The following list is from that classroom

TABLE 5-1 Selected Categories of Words

Specific Words	Descriptive Words	Parts of Speech	Sequence Words
names	something that happened	verbs	causes
places	important events	adjectives	prior events
times	emotions	nouns	sizes
colors	things seen	prepositional phrases	ages
objects	things felt		
movable items	things heard		
odors	big events		
tangible items	feelings		
key words	things that move		
sight words	nice things		
words with suffixes	pretty things		
transportation			
contractions			

and is included in this chapter to emphasize the impact a variety of stories can make to the kindergarten year. The categories of words are also included to illustrate the importance of changing the category daily.

This list is not a "required" list of books to read to kindergarten students. Another pilot kindergarten teacher preferred to start the year with Dr. Seuss books. While reading the list of titles and the corresponding word categories, note the tremendous amount of knowledge that students will be exposed to in an indirect fashion as they listen to the stories.

LESSON	WORD CATEGORY EMPHASIZED	BOOK
1	character names	Felix Salten, **Bambi,** Golden Press, 1973.
2	places	Jean De Brunhoff, **The Story of Babar,** Random House, 1960.
3	verbs	Maurice Sendak, **Where the Wild Things Are,** Harper & Row
4	names	Philippe and Rejane Fix, **The Pink Elephant with Golden Spots,** Golden Press, 1971.
5	adjectives	Adelaide Holl, **Sylvester the Mouse with the Musical Ear,** Golden Press, 1973.
6	times	Retold by Janet Fulton from a French text by Anne-Marie Dalmais, **The Adventures of Little Rabbit: A Day with Little Rabbit,** Golden Press, 1972.
7	words for something that happened	H. A. Ray, **Curious George,** Houghton Mifflin, 1969.
8	names	Irma Joyce, **Never Talk to Strangers,** Golden Press, 1972.
9	something that caused something to happen	Story adapted by Jane Werner, **Snow White and the Seven Dwarfs,** Golden Press, 1974.
10	descriptions	Retold by Janet Fulton from a French text by Anne-Marie Dalmais, **The Adventures of Little Rabbit: The Adventures in the Garden,** Golden Press, 1972.
11	character names	Sir James M. Barrie, **Peter Pan,** Golden Press, 1973.
12	colors	Alice and Martin Provensen, **What Is a Color?** Golden Press, 1967.
13	important events	Jane Pilgrim, **Henry Goes Visiting,** Brockhampton Press, 1972.
14	sight words	Richard Scarry, **Going Places,** Golden Press, 1971.

LESSON	WORD CATEGORY EMPHASIZED	BOOK
15	names of places	Anne Carriere, **Jennifer's Walk**, Golden Press, 1973.
16	objects	Robert Bright, **Georgie**, Scholastic Book Services, 1944.
17	movable items	Richard Scarry, **The Great Big Car and Truck Book**, Golden Press, 1974.
18	emotions	Retold by Janet Fulton from a French text by Anne-Marie Dalmais, **The Adventures of Little Rabbit: An Adventure in the Snow**, Golden Press, 1972.
19	things that are seen	Retold by Annemarie Colbin from a French text by Anne-Marie Dalmais, **The Adventures of Brownie and Puff: Brownie and Puff**, Golden Press, 1971.
20	things that are felt	Donna Lugg Pape, **Mary Lou the Kangaroo**, E.M. Hale and Company, 1968.
21	things that have odors	Katherine Howard, **Max the Nosey Bear**, Golden Press, 1972.
22	things that are heard	Richard Scarry, **Going Places**, Golden Press, 1971.
23	character names	Retold by Janet Fulton from a French text by Anne-Marie Dalmais, **The Adventures of Little Rabbit: The Adventure of the Stretched-Out Dog**, Golden Press, 1972.
24	different sizes	Caroline Kramer, **The Three Billy Goats Gruff**, Random House, 1957.
25	sight words	Noah Smaridge, **Litterbugs Come in Every Size**, Golden Press, 1972.
26	funny words	Caroline Kramer, **The Three Little Pigs**, from **Read-Aloud Nursery Tales**, Random House, 1957.
27	colors	A.A. Milne, Adapted by Norm McGary and Bill Lorencz, **Winnie-the-Pooh and Eeyore's Birthday**, Golden Press, 1974.
28	adjectives	Retold by Annemarie Colbin from a French text by Anne-Marie Dalmais, **The Adventures of Brownie and Puff: Brownie and Puff at the Beach**, Golden Press, 1971.
29	verbs	Walt Disney Productions, **Robin Hood**, Golden Press, 1973.

LESSON	WORD CATEGORY EMPHASIZED	BOOK
30	names of places	Bryon Preiss, **The Silent E's from Outer Space**, Western Publishing, 1973.
31	character ages	P. D. Eastman, **Are You My Mother?** Random House, 1960.
32	things that are seen	Beatrix Potter, **The Tale of Peter Rabbit**, Golden Press, 1973.
33	character names	David L. Harrison, **Piggy Wiglet and the Great Adventure**, Golden Press, 1973.
34	words denoting time	Sune Engelbrekston, **"The Sun is a Star"** from **Sounds Around the Clock** by Bill Martin, Jr., Holt, Rinehart and Winston, 1966.
35	sight words	Herbert McClure, **Children of the World Say "Good Morning,"** Holt, Rinehart and Winston, 1963.
36	emotions	Ariane, **The Lively Little Rabbit**, Golden Press, 1973.
37	descriptions	Patricia K. Miller and Iran L. Seligman, **"Big Frogs, Little Frogs,"** from **Sounds Around the Clock** by Bill Martin, Jr., Holt, Rinehart and Winston, 1966.
38	items in the story	Eloise Wilkin, **The Baby Book**, Golden Press, 1973.
39	verbs	Little Golden Books, **The Poky Little Puppy**, Golden Press, 1972.
40	common nouns	Kathleen Leverich, **Cricket's Expeditions**, Random House, 1977.
41	things that are heard	Paul Showers, **The Listening Walk**, Crowell, 1961.
42	character names	Rudyard Kipling, **The Jungle Book**, Random House, 1974.
43	verbs	Patsy Scarry, **Pierre Bear, My Nursery Tale Book**, Golden Press, 1974.
44	nouns	Marjorie Flack, **Ask Mr. Bear**, Macmillan, 1932.
45	sight words	Mary McBurney Green, **When Will I Whistle?** F. Watts, 1967.
46	adjectives	Mae and Ira Freeman, **You Will Go To the Moon**, Random House, 1959.

LESSON	WORD CATEGORY EMPHASIZED	BOOK
47	names of places in the story	Virginia Lee Burton, **Mike Mulligan and His Steam Shovel**, Houghton Mifflin, 1939.
48	words denoting size	Charlotte Zolotow, **Big Sister and Little Sister**, Harper & Row, 1966.
49	feelings mentioned in the story	Claire Hucket Bishop, **The Five Chinese Brothers**, Coward-McCann, 1938.
50	words ending in *ed*	Crusby Bunsall, **The Case of the Hungry Stranger**, Harper & Row, 1963.
51	words ending in *ing*	John Burningham, **Mr. Gumpy's Outing**, Holt, 1971.
52	sight words	Dick Martin, **The Sand Pail Book**, Golden Press, 1964.
53	colors	Marjorie Weinman Sharmat, **A Big, Fat Enormous Lie**, Dutton, 1978.
54	character names	Norah Smaridge, **Raggedy Andy**, Golden Press, 1973.
55	adjectives	Robyn Supraner, **It's Not Fair**, Warne, 1976.
56	nouns	Feodor Rojankovsky, **The Great Big Wild Animal Book**, Golden Press, 1951.
57	words with suffixes	Rex Parkin, **The Shadow Train**, Macmillan, 1962.
58	silly parts in the story	Marjorie Flack, **The Boats on the River**, Viking, 1946.
59	words with prefixes	Ivar Myrhoj, **Pondus the Penguin**, Golden Press, 1968.
60	emotions	Kathryn Lasky, **Tugboats Never Sleep**, Little Brown, 1977.
61	objects	Jane Werner Watson, **The True Story of Smokey the Bear**, Golden Press, 1955.
62	sight words	Nathaniel Benchley, **Red Fox and His Canoe**, Harper & Row, 1964.
63	prepositional phrases	H. A. Rey, **Curious George Gets a Medal**, Houghton Mifflin, 1957.
64	places	Adelaide Holl, **Little Dog Lost**, Western Publishing, 1970.

LESSON	WORD CATEGORY EMPHASIZED	BOOK
65	description of a character	Janet Deering, **Eddie's Moving Day**, Golden Press, 1970.
66	funny words	Edith Thatcher Hurd, **Hurry, Hurry**, Harper & Row, 1960.
67	description of places	Ruth G. Gilroy and Frank O. Gilroy, **Little Ego**, Simon and Schuster, 1970.
68	description of objects	Pictures by Esme Eve, **Birds**, Wonder Books, 1973.
69	sight words	Norman Bridwell, **Clifford's Good Deeds**, Four Winds Press, 1975.
70	verbs	Walter Farley, **Little Black Goes to the Circus**, Random House, 1963.
71	numbers	Mary Reed and Edith Osswald, **Numbers**, Golden Press, 1955.
72	things that move	William Dugan, **The Car Book**, Golden Press, 1971.
73	adjectives	Marjorie Flack, **Angus and the Ducks**, Doubleday, 1930.
74	verbs	Helen Palmer, **I Was Kissed by a Seal at the Zoo**, Random House, 1962.
75	colors	Millicent E. Selsam, **Tony's Birds**, Harper & Row, 1961.
76	descriptions	Dr. Seuss, **The Cat in the Hat**, Random House, 1957.
77	words denoting time	Peggy Parish, **Amelia Bedelia and the Surprise Shower**, Harper & Row, 1966.
78	words about the environment	Pearl Wolf, **Gorilla Baby: The Story of Patty Cake**, Scholastic Book Services, 1974.
79	character names	Charlotte Zolotow, **Mr. Rabbit and the Lovely Present**, Harper & Row, 1962.
80	words denoting emotions	Robert Bright, **Georgie and the Robbers**, Doubleday, 1963.
81	important words	Ellen Raskin, **Nothing Ever Happens on My Block**, Atheneum, 1967.

LESSON	WORD CATEGORY EMPHASIZED	BOOK
82	characters	Bill Peet, **Randy's Dandy Lions**, Houghton Mifflin, 1964.
83	places	Patricia M. Scarry, **The Golden Story Book of River Bend; Welcome to River Bend**, Golden Press, 1969.
84	transportation words	Watty Piper, **The Little Engine That Could**, Platt and Munk, 1961.
85	references to food	Eve Rice, **Papa's Lemonade and Other Stories**, Greenwillow Books, 1976.
86	words denoting size	Rosamond Daver, **Bullfrog Grows Up**, Greenwillow Brooks, 1976.
87	words denoting places	Margaret Wise Brown, **The Runaway Bunny**, Harper & Row, 1970.
88	sight words	Ezra Jack Keats, **Pet Show**, Macmillan, 1972.
89	emotions indicated	Charles M. Schulz, **It's a Mystery, Charlie Brown**, Random House, 1975.
90	adjectives	Ezra Jack Keats, **The Snowy Day**, Scholastic Book Services, 1962.
91	objects	__________, **Humpty Dumpty's Holiday Stories**, Parents' Magazine Press, 1973.
92	verbs	May Garelick, **What Makes a Bird a Bird?** Follett, 1969.
93	character names	Nonny Hogrogian, **One Fine Day**, Macmillan, 1971.
94	sight words	Naomi John White Sellers, **Charley's Clan**, Albert Whitman, 1973.
95	nice things	Arthur Getz, **Hamilton Duck's Springtime Story**, Golden Press, 1974.
96	prepositional phrases	Eugene H. Hippopotamus, **Hello Hippopotamus**, Simon & Schuster, 1969.
97	something pretty	Robert McCloskey, **Burt Dow-Deepwater Man**, Viking Press, 1963.
98	objects	Helen and Alf Evers, **So Long**, Rand McNally, 1957.

LESSON	WORD CATEGORY EMPHASIZED	BOOK
99	places	Mieko Maeda, **How Rabbit Tricked His Friends,** Parents' Magazine Press, 1969.
100	events in the story	Retold by Stella Williams Nathan, **Chicken Little,** Whitman, 1966.
101	rhyming words	Dr. Seuss, **Hop on Pop**, Random House, 1963.
102	emotions	Mildred Kantrowitz, **Maxie**, Parent's Magazine Press, 1970.
103	words ending in *ed*	Ruth Belou Gross, **What is That Alligator Saying?** Scholastic Book Services, 1974.
104	adjectives	A.A. Milne, **The House at Pooh Corner**, Dell, 1928.
105	colors	Ruth Wilson, **Outdoor Wonderland,** Lothrop, Lee and Shepard, 1961.
106	sight words	Julia Cunningham, **Macaroon,** Pantheon Books, 1962.
107	exciting words	Miriam Young, **So What if it's Raining!** Parent's Magazine Press, 1976.
108	animal names	Margaret Mahy, **Ultra-Violet Catastrophe,** Parent's Magazine Press, 1975.
109	verbs	Mary Calhoun, **Old Man Whickutt's Donkey,** Parent's Magazine Press, 1975.
110	nouns	Mike Thaler, **How Far Will a Rubber Band Stretch?** Parent's Magazine Press, 1974.
111	prepositional phrases	A.A. Milne, **Three Stories from Winnie-the-Pooh,** Scholastic Book Services, 1926.
112	character names	Franklyn M. Branley and Eleanor K. Vaughan, **Mickey's Magnet**, Scholastic Book Services, 1926.
113	things that are heard	Miriam Young, **Miss Susy**, Parent's Magazine Press, 1964.
114	silly parts in the story	Beatrix Potter, **The Tale of Squirrel Nutkin**, Warne, 1903.
115	places	Alice O'Grady and Frances Throup, **The Cap that Mother Made,** Rand McNally, 1957.

LESSON	WORD CATEGORY EMPHASIZED	BOOK
116	contractions	Eleanor Clymer, **Chipmunk in the Forest**, Atheneum, 1965.
117	adjectives describing people	Mircea Vasiliu, **Mortimer, the Friendly Dragon**, John Day, 1968.
118	sight words	Beatrix Potter, **The Tale of Mr. Jeremy Fisher**, Warne, 1934.
119	exciting parts of the story	Millicent E. Selsam, **Terry and the Caterpillars**, Harper & Row, 1962.
120	something sad	Anne Rockwell, **The Gollywhopper Egg**, Macmillan, 1974.
121	words ending in *ing*	Lillian Moore, **Little Raccoon amd the Thing in the Pool**, Scholastic Book Services, 1963.
122	adjectives	Lisl Weil, **Walt and Pepper**, Parent's Magazine Press, 1974.
123	numbers	Jane Yolen, **An Invitation to the Butterfly Ball**, Parents' Magazine Press, 1976.
124	things that are heard	Phyllis La Farge, **Granny's Fish Story**, Parents' Magazine Press, 1975.
125	words denoting time	Bernard Waber, **Lovable Lyle**, Houghton Mifflin, 1969.
126	exciting words	Fernando Krahn, **The Family Minus**, Parents' Magazine Press, 1977.
127	adjectives describing places	A.A. Milne, **Three Stories from Winnie-the-Pooh**, Scholastic Book Services, 1926.
128	words ending in *ed*	Arnold Lobel, **Frog and Toad Together**, Scholastic Book Services, 1971.
129	movable items	Nancy Faulkner, **Small Clown**, Doubleday, 1960.
130	important events	Told to Charles L. Blood and Martin Link by Geraldine, **The Goat in the Rug**, Parents' Magazine Press, 1976.
131	emotions	Shan Ellentuck, **A Sunflower as Big as the Sun**, Doubleday, 1968.

LESSON	WORD CATEGORY EMPHASIZED	BOOK
132	places	Richard Scarry, **Going Places**, Golden Press, 1971.
133	number of characters in the story.	A.A. Milne, **Three Stories from Winnie-the-Pooh,** Scholastic Book Services, 1926.
134	sentences in the story	William E. Jones and Minerva J. Goldberg, **Going to Kindergarten,** Oddo, 1968.
135	verbs	Donna K. Grasuenor, **Zoo Babies**, National Geographic Society, 1978.
136	words ending in *ing*	Katherine Howard, **Little Bunny Follows His Nose,** Golden Press, 1971.
137	sight words	Carl Memling, **Ride, Willy, Ride,** Follett, 1970.
138	words denoting time	Richard Scarry, **Things to Know,** Golden Press, 1971.
139	sequence of events	Retold by Evelyn Andreas, **Cinderella,** Wonder Books, 1954.
140	modes of transportation	Beatrix Scharen, **Gigin and Till,** Atheneum, 1968.
141	colors in the story	P. D. Eastman, **Go, Dog, Go!** Random House, 1961.
142	character names	Traudl, **Kostas the Rooster,** Lothrop, Lee & Shephard, 1968.
143	emotions	Mary J. Fulton, **My Friend,** Golden Press, 1973.
144	unhappy characters	A. K. Roche, **The Pumpkin Heads,** Prentice-Hall, 1968.
145	exciting parts of the story	Based on original story by Sterling North, **The Runaway Lamb at the County Fair,** Grosset and Dunlap, 1948.
146	funny words	Steward Beach, **Good Morning Sun's Up!** Scroll Press, 1968.
147	happy parts in the story	Jean Craighead George, **The Moon of the Bears,** Crowell, 1967.
148	colors	___________, **Read-Aloud Romper Room Stories,** Wonder Books, 1958.
149	verbs	Virginia Lee Burton, **Calico the Wonder Horse,** Scholastic Book Services, 1950.

LESSON	WORD CATEGORY EMPHASIZED	BOOK
150	important parts in the story	Edna Walker Chandler, **Cowboy Andy**, Random House, 1959.
151	something pretty	Marjorie Barrow, **The Funny Hat**, Rand McNally, 1959.
152	nicest persons in the story	Mary Carey, **The Rubbles and Bamm-Bamm Problem Present**, Whitman, 1965.
153	happiest characters	___________, **Big Big Story Book**, Whitman, 1961.
154	adjectives	Caroline Emerson, **Make Way for the Thruway**, Golden Press, 1961.
155	exciting parts	___________, **"Ali Baba and the Forty Thieves,"** from **A Thousand and One Arabian Nights**, Simon and Schuster, 1958.
156	sight words	Gene Darby, **What is a Frog?** Scholastic Book Services, 1957.
157	objects in the story	___________, **Humpty Dumpty's Holiday Stories**, Parents' Magazine Press, 1973.
158	emotions	Leo Dorfman, **Twinkles and Sanford's Boat**, Whitman, 1962.
159	places in the story	Anna and Edward C. Stardon, **Birdie the Bantam**, Dial, 1967.
160	items in the story	Carolyn Sherwin Bailey, **The Little Rabbit Who Wanted Red Wings**, Platt and Munk, 1954.
161	main characters	___________, **Read-Aloud Romper Room Stories**, Wonder Books, 1958.
162	places	Mary and Conrad Bluff, **Hurry, Skurry, and Flurry**, The Junior Literacy Guild, 1954.
163	prepositional phrases	Retold by Caroline Kramer, **Read-Aloud Nursery Tales**, Random House, 1957.
164	words ending in plural *s*	Marjorie Flack, **The Boats on the River**, Viking, 1956.
165	words ending in *ing*	Retold by Caroline Kramer, **Read-Aloud Nursery Tales**, Random House, 1957.

LESSON	WORD CATEGORY EMPHASIZED	BOOK
166	silly words	Eleanore Schmid, **Tonia,** G.P. Putnam's Sons, 1970.
167	things that are seen	**Mary Poppins,** based on the Walt Disney Motion Picture, adapted by Annie North Bedford, Golden Press, 1964.
168	verbs	Jane Thayer, **Curious, Furious Chipmunk,** Morrow, 1969.
169	final events	Margit Raedel, **Timpetoo,** Carolrhoda Books, 1971.
170	sight words	___________, **Big Big Story Book,** Whitman, 1961.
171	occupations	Irwin Shapiro, **Twice Upon a Time,** Xerox Family Education Services, 1973.
172	funny words	Garry and Vesta Smith, **Crickety Cricket,** Steck-Vaughn, 1969.
173	words for feelings	Ruth Van Wess Blair, **A Bear Can Hibernate—Why Can't I?** T. S. Denison and Company, 1972.
174	sad words	Ludwig Bemelmans, **Madeline in London,** Viking, 1961.
175	nouns	Ada Litchfield, **The Wonderful Wonderful Book,** Steck-Vaughn, 1968.
176	nice feelings in the story	Margaret Bloy Graham, **Benjy's Dog House,** Harper & Row, 1973.
177	adjectives	Retold by Aliki, **The Eggs,** Pantheon Books, 1969.
178	words related to time	Sara Asheron, **Little Gray Mouse Goes Sailing,** Wonder Books, 1965.
179	verbs	Vera Kistiakowsky Fischer, **One Way is Down,** Little, Brown, 1967.
180	exciting words	Peggy Mann, **The Boy with a Billion Pets,** Coward-McCann, 1968.

Some children enter kindergarten reading and writing, while others learn during their kindergarten year. For example, one student may enter kindergarten reading on the fifth grade level; another kindergarten student may not be reading at all by the end of the academic year.

Arrange with the school librarian for at least 40 library books in the kindergarten class to be exchanged every two weeks for different books. The books should range from picture books to stories with no pictures. Some kindergarten students like to read no-picture stories. Provide time when all children—readers and nonreaders—have opportunities to look through the books.

The principal of one kindergarten class visited the class during the "rest time" period. Most of the students were quietly looking at a library book while they were "resting."

Kindergarten classes should have regularly scheduled times to go to the library and check out books. Because there will be times when an individual wants to know more about a particular topic, the library policy should be flexible enough to allow that child, even though he or she is in the kindergarten, to go to the librarian and ask for help in locating books on the topic.

Kindergartners should experience a year in which reading and writing are an enjoyable part of the daily curriculum with the daily exposure element overriding pressure or fragmented incidental instruction. The number of hours in each school day remains the same; what happens during those hours can significantly change the program offered to youngsters.

The *Success in Kindergarten Reading and Writing* program provides a base structure that each teacher can implement according to his or her expertise and professional judgment. The *Success* program is not simply a collection of isolated activities.

The four modules of the *Success* program, taught daily, provide four different approaches to reading and writing readiness. It is easy to correlate the modules; yet, each adds its own distinctive dimension and enjoyment to the instructional program. Horizontally, the correlation appears when one aspect introduced in one module is noticed and reinforced informally in a different module on the same day. Vertically, the correlation appears when an item or topic introduced in one module is incorporated into a module later in the year.

The *Success* program provides a combination of structure and creative flexibility, which is part of the readiness concept of the future. This combination can help provide educationally sound kindergarten programs that give students opportunities to learn to read and write and opportunities to feel good about the reading and writing process before they enter first grade.

chapter six
Information for Parents

Before the *Success* program was published, many parents asked the authors how they could help their child at home. Other parents asked what they could do at home to supplement or reinforce what the child was learning at school. The authors' responses had to be fairly general, with replies such as "read to your child," and a host of other traditional suggestions.

With the publication of this book a void is filled. This chapter is written especially for parents to use either independently at home, if the child is not being taught the *Success* program in kindergarten, or to coordinate help at home with the kinds of instruction offered in *Success* classes at school. Obviously, there are many other activities that both teacher and parents will offer the child; however, the *Success* program affords a long overdue vehicle for both parents and teachers to use to bring their efforts closer together and provide continuity and reinforcement.

This chapter condenses for parents the basic theories and methodology suggestions of the preceding chapters. The emphasis is on a home-based rather than a school-based program.

The authors recommend that parents ask for a conference with their child's kindergarten teacher and plan together how they can best use the *Success* program with the overall purpose of jointly providing an excellent preschool program for the child.

Figure 6–1 is an example of one teacher's letter to parents. Note that the teacher listed specific topics/skills that were discussed in the classroom and encouraged parents to become involved in the child's educational process.

The *Success* program can easily be adapted for use by parents with children at home. By incorporating the child's vocabulary, printed words from familiar items in the child's home environment, and a flexible instruction structure, the *Success* program exposes the child to reading and writing instruction in a positive way. There is no predetermined developmental sequence that each child must fit into; rather, the reading and writing instruction is incorporated with the developmental process of each child. The modules of the *Success* program are designed so that reading and writing are as natural to the child as playing and speaking.

The parent should *not* pressure the child during any of the modules. An informal, relaxed atmosphere will provide opportunities for parent-child interaction while offering necessary readiness skills. Mastery is *not* the major concept, but rather, exposure to a wide variety of printed materials related to the needs of the individual child.

Readiness skills within the modules *do not have to be taught at any particular time or at any particular place during the day.* The Alphabet Module, for example, could be taught at the

News from Room 409 February 16, 1979

The best plans in the world can't prevent a snowstorm! We are planning to go to the airport on March 8 unless something else happens.

Our valentine exchange went pretty well on Wednesday even though I had to be out of school again (a death in my family). The children were really excited about their valentines and seemed to enjoy giving them as much as receiving them.

This week we talked about Abraham Lincoln and about how important it is to be honest. We will continue this next week when we talk about George Washington.

Our Success program is going very well! Ask your child about these things:

1. nouns
2. verbs
3. helping verbs
4. apostrophe s
5. phrases
6. sentences

Our rhyming words this week were: phone, map, rake, and steer. Please review these with your child. Remember, words do not have to be spelled exactly alike to rhyme. For example all these words rhyme:

steer
deer
tear } notice the difference in the
fear } spelling of these words.
cheer

Help your child sound out rhyming words and if he still wants to do more, then help him write them. Be sure to point out the difference in the spelling if you write them.

Thank to those who sent in Kleenex. It surely has helped!

FIGURE 6-1 Example of a Teacher's Letter to Parents

breakfast table one morning or before bedtime the next day. The Story Time Module could be taught during mid-morning or at bedtime. Flexibility is the key and parents should make the sessions as informal and as pressure-free as possible.

Informal reinforcement for any of the modules can take place almost anywhere. For example, a child might be asked to find a certain letter that has been discussed during the Alphabet Module on a cereal box or a milk carton.

We suggest that each module last for only a few minutes. A range of four fifteen-minutes segments is appropriate depending on the specific lesson and the time and place the lesson is being taught. Do not expect the child to learn a particular letter or word at a particular time. In all probability, that child will encounter that letter and word many, many times during his or her life. Gradually, over a period of time, the learning takes place.

THE PICTURE/WORD ASSOCIATION MODULE

The major purposes of the Picture/Word Association Module are to provide opportunities for the child to (1) volunteer his or her words associated with a variety of pictures, (2) observe the formation of each letter within the words as it is written by the parent and (3) possibly, read the words. It is extremely important that the *child*, not the parent, volunteer the words used in this module.

How to Teach the Picure/Word Association Module

1. The parent and/or child locates or draws a picture related to the suggested theme found in the second column of a lesson in Appendix One. For example, if the theme is *automobile tires*, the picture could be a full page magazine advertisement about a particular car for sale. In the picture, there would be *tires* on the car. The picture should have *much detail* in it. A picture depicting only *tires* should not be used.

2. The picture should be taped in the center of a sheet of paper. The child should sit beside the parent.

3. The parent briefly discusses the picture with the child.

4. The parent asks the child to think of a title for the picture, and writes that title on the paper above the picture. At first, the parent will need to guide the selection of titles, but as the lessons progress, the child will be able to select titles independently. The parent should call attention to the fact that important words in the title begin with a capital letter. At first, this will have little meaning for the child. As the lessons progress, the child learns this informally.

The parent says the *name* of each letter *as it is written* and asks the child to say the letter name as it is written or as he or she hears it pronounced. The parent should not wait to say the letter names after the word is written. *The sound of any letter in* the Picture/Word Association Module should not be emphasized. One concept the child learns is the association of letter symbols with the names of the letters.

The object is *not* to isolate any of the thousands of sound combinations within words or to dwell on the particular sound of one or two particular sounds.

5. The child is asked to point to one item in the picture and say its name. The parent writes the words volunteered, *voicing the name of each letter as it is written*. The child says the names of the letters as they are written or as he/she hears the parent say them. Then the entire word is pronounced.

6. The child draws a line from the item in the picture to the word written on the paper.

7. The same procedure is followed for some of the other items in the picture. The lessons should not tire the child, and they should be enjoyable to both parent and child.

Soon the child will want to write. The parent shows the child how to form a part of a letter within a word—for example, the horizontal line on the letter *t*. The child should not be forced to write, however. As the child learns to write letters or parts of letters, he or she should write those items and tell the parent the name of the letter. As the lessons progress, with the reinforcement from the Alphabet Module, the child learns to write. The parent helps with spelling the words.

8. After Lesson 20, the parent can help the child develop a sentence that contains *some* of the words written on the paper. The sentence is written at the bottom of the page, the parent commenting about capitalization and punctuation. The child then "reads" the sentence orally with the parent as each word in the sentence is touched. This procedure is continued with each lesson to help the child develop a title for the picture.

9. If possible, some of the papers should be displayed somewhere in the house—on a wall or on the refrigerator. As new Picture/Word Association papers are completed, they can replace the previous ones.

The child will, from time to time, respond to the displayed papers without any coaxing from the parent. This is one of the built-in reinforcers incorporated into the *Success* program.

10. Chapter Two has an explanation of various Phases in the Picture/Word Association Module. Figures 2-1 through 2-6 are examples of charts developed in a school kindergarten class during the Picture/Word Association Module. The number of words written at home during this module will vary from day to day, depending on the interest span of the child.

THE ALPHABET MODULE

The purposes of the Alphabet Module include introducing the child to the writing of symbols of the English language and the noting of selected sounds of letter combinations in ways that are correlated with language development, art, object association, listening, and rhyming.

The third column in Appendix One suggests sequences and emphases.

No child should be made to form an alphabet symbol correctly or "draw" an adult rendition of a horse; however, the child can be helped to create a part of a letter or a part of a horse.

The child will need unlined paper, regular-sized pencils with erasers, crayons, and something to file his or her papers in, such as a manila folder or notebook. Lined paper is used only after the child can form letter symbols with some degree of legibility and has developed the concept of spacing between letters and words.

The parent should comment positively on some part of a letter a child has attempted and show how some part could be improved. The parent should not adopt a sense of urgency for the child to suddenly become proficient in letter formation. There is plenty of time. It is best if the child enjoys *trying* to make the letter symbols rather than worry about pleasing the parent. By correlating the writing of letters with art activities, a child has a chance to enjoy learning to write and to improve his or her writing abilities.

How to Teach the Alphabet Module

1. The module emphasis is introduced for example, in Lesson 1, the emphasis is the letter *l*. If there is a chalkboard in the home, it can be used to illustrate how to form the letter *l* and the child can be asked to practice making the letter in the air. If no chalkboard is available (and it is not necessary to have one), a piece of unlined paper can be used.

2. The child completes an art project, for example, drawing his or her own drawing of an item or coloring a picture, and practices making *l*'s on the drawing according to his or her ability.

3. The child's paper should be dated and filed. This longitudinal record provides opportunities for the child and parent to see the progress that has been made. As the child learns to date the paper, he or she should be encouraged to do so.

Chapter Three has a detailed explanation of the eight developmental Phases in the Alphabet Module. In Phase VI—Object Labeling—objects in the home should be substituted for the suggested objects in the classroom.

THE ORAL LANGUAGE/READING MODULE

The Oral Language/Reading Module incorporates the spoken vocabulary of the child with the observation of the writing and reading of words; however, the methodology of teaching is different from that used in the Picture/Word Association Module.

The suggested themes are found in the fourth column of each lesson. The parent should change the module's theme if it is not appropriate for a particular day or if something has happened that would indicte a theme of greater immediate interest to the child—for example, a birthday party.

How to Teach the Oral Language/ Reading Module

There are three basic procedures in teaching the Oral Language/Reading Module:

1. The parent discusses briefly with the child a particular theme. For example, the theme suggested for Lesson 1 is *toys*. The parent might ask which toys are the child's favorite and why.

2. Using a Magic Marker, the parent writes *one* word spoken by the child and his or her name on a small strip of paper. For example, a child

might respond, "I like Freddy the dog because he is so soft." The word *dog* could be written on the strip of paper.

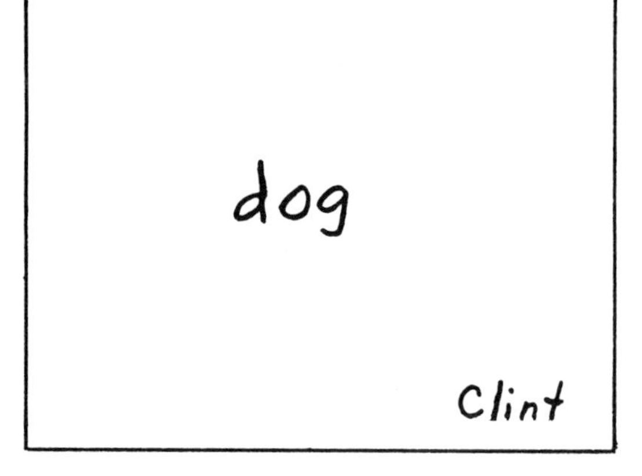

The parent *says the letter names as each is written: d-o-g,* and writes the child's name on the strip of paper.

3. The child displays the strip of paper somewhere in the house, such as on a bulletin board, on the refrigerator, or on a door. The child may wish to glue the strip of paper on notebook paper and keep the strips in a notebook. Words written on strips of paper can be used later as reviews and/or reinforcements if the parent decides to do so. For example, the strip of paper with the word *dog* written on it can be used as a review of letter recognition. *The child* should not be required or expected *to memorize the word.*

There are three Phases in the Oral Language/Reading Module. Phase I (Lessons 1-80) emphasizes single words spoken by the child. Phase II (Lessons 81-100) emphasizes picture/word cluster associations. Phase III (Lessons 101-180) emphasizes sentences containing a specific word cluster. (A word cluster is any group of words, not necessarily a sentence.)

Suggested Procedure for Teaching Phase I

1. The suggested theme listed in the fourth column of the lessons is discussed or a more appropriate theme to the child is selected. For example, if the child has just received new shoes, the theme could be changed to *shoes.* The child is asked what he or she likes best about the shoes, where they might travel, etc. The response might be, "I like the red color best of all." On a strip of paper, the words *red color* and the child's name are written.

red color

Clint

The name of each letter is said as it is being written. The parent should make sure the child observes the writing of his or her word and should encourage the child to help name the letters.

3. The child displays the strip of paper somewhere in the house, preferably a space the child can call his or her own. Strips can also be glued to paper and kept in a notebook.

Puppets can be used to encourage the child to talk about various themes. Small paper bags or socks can be used if parents do not want to buy puppets. Puppets provide the child with opportunities to pretend and engage in conversation at the same time. The parent should use a puppet also, and the word(s) written will be some of those "spoken" by the puppet the child uses.

The conversation during the Oral Language/Reading Module should be guided so the theme of the writing relates to at least one recognizable topic, which may or may not be the theme suggested in the lesson. It is important to include a variety of themes during this module.

Suggested Procedure for Teaching Phase II

1. The suggested theme is discussed or the theme is changed if necessary.

2. The child is asked to locate a picture in a magazine or catalog that *he or she can associate with that theme or topic.* At least one *word cluster* spoken by the child and his or her name are written

on or near the picture. The picture may need to be glued on notebook paper or some other paper and the words written on that paper so they will be visible. For example, the theme suggested for Lesson 94 is *trucks*. The child might find a magazine picture with a truck in it, and during the discussion respond, "The truck is carrying lots of wood. It is a big truck." The parent then may write the following word cluster, *lots of wood, big truck*.

3. The parent or the child writes at least one word cluster spoken by the child associated with the picture.

4. The child displays his or her picture and word cluster.

Suggested Procedure for Teaching Phase III

1. The suggested theme is discussed or the theme is changed if necessary. In Appendix One, there is a suggested word cluster that can be used as a reference point in each lesson. For example, in Lesson 163, the cluster is *watching a game*. The parent might ask, "What do you see when you watch a game?" If the child responds, "I see people win," the parent might write on the strip of paper, "Billy sees people win." The exact word cluster suggested for Lessons 101–180 does not have to be included in the sentence that is written on the strip of paper.

2. The parent or the child writes a sentence spoken by the child.

3. The child may draw, color, or paint a picture associated with the sentence written. For example, in Lesson 163, the child might draw basketball players winning a game.

4. The child displays his or her sentence and art work. The parent should not pressure the child during the Oral Language/Reading Module. The module offers opportunities for parent and child to interact while correlating reading, writing, listening, thinking, spelling, grammar, and art in a structure according to a theme, yet providing a flexible readiness program.

THE STORY TIME MODULE

Many parents read stories to children. The Story Time Module incorporates the reading of a story with word categories for children to see, but not necessarily to read.

The major purpose of the Story Time Module is to provide listening experiences with a large number of different books in an informal, relaxed atmosphere.

How to Teach the Story Time Module

1. A book is selected and three or four words are written on a piece of paper. These words should relate to the category of words suggested in the fifth column of a lesson.

During Phase I, words are written *before* the story is read. During Phase II (Lessons 101–180) words are written either *before* or *after* the story is read. For example, in Lesson 11, the word category is *character names*. The parent may wish to read the story of Peter Pan and write the following words: *Peter Pan, Wendy, Captain Hook, Tinkerbell.*

2. The parent sits with the child and reads the selected story. *Occasionally*, as one of the words or word clusters written on the paper is read from the book, the parent places a hand under the word to call attention to it. This is a *brief* pause and should not interrupt the flow of the story.

3. Games using the words, such as finding certain letters, finding letters in the child's name or other family names, and discussions of the story are optional activities the parent can include in the Story Time Module.

The piece of paper containing the words or word clusters can be displayed by the child somewhere in the house, filed, or thrown away. Stories read at other times during the day should not incorporate the word category component of the Story Time Module.

The Phases in the Story Time Module

Phase I includes Lessons 1–100. As indicated earlier, the words or word clusters are written on a piece of paper before the story is read to the child.

Phase II incorporates Lessons 101–180. The words are written before or after the story is read. For example, the parent can locate some words associated with colors in the story and write some of those on a piece of paper before the story is read. On the other hand, writing words associated with main characters in the story (Lesson 161) might best be accomplished through a discussion after the story is read. In both phases, the child *sees* words written in a form different from the printed version he or she *hears* in the story and sees in printed form.

A list of suggested books to use during the Story Time Module is found in Chapter Five. This list is a *suggestion* and does not imply that these are the only books that could or should be used.

A list of suggested categories emphasized in the Story Time Module is also found in Chapter Five, and in the fifth column in Appendix One. Parents can change the categories they wish, however it is very important that they offer a variety of word categories, rather than select limited kinds of words.

Each time the parent and child team together during the modules in a *Success* lesson, much more takes place than aspects of the reading/writing process. These are special times for sharing and mutual enjoyment, and should not be missed.

References

The following references are suggested for activities ideas:

Adams, Anne H. *The Clock Struck One.* San Rafael, Calif.: Leswing Press, 1973.

Adams, Ruth J. *Creative Woodwork in the Kindergarten.* Minneapolis: Dennison, 1963.

Allen, Roach Val, and Allen, Claryce. *Language Experiences in Early Childhood: A Teacher's Resource Book.* Chicago: Encyclopedia Britannica Press, 1969.

Baumer, Mary P. *Seasonal Kindergarten Units.* Belmont, Calif.: Fearon, 1972.

Berry, James C., and Treadway, Charles F. *Kindergarten Resource Book.* Nashville, Tenn.: Broadman Press, 1965.

Berry, Paulette, et. al. *Kindergarten Kapers: 13 Units of Study for Early Childhood.* Minneapolis: Dennison, 1976.

Blake, Jim, and Ernst, Barbara. *The Great Perpetual Learning Machine: Being a Stupendous Collection of Ideas, Games, Experiments, Activities, and Recommendations for Further Exploration with Tons of Illustrations.* Boston: Little, Brown, 1976.

Brono, Janet, and Dackan, Peggy. *Cooking in the Classroom.* Belmont, Calif.: Fearon, 1974.

Cochran, Norman A., et. al. *Learning on the Move: An Activity Guide for Preschool Parents and Teachers.* Dubuque, Iowa: Kendall/Hunt, 1975.

Collier, Mary Jo; Forte, Imogene, and MacKenzie, Joy. *Kid's Stuff: Kindergarten and Nursery School.* Nashville, Tenn.: Incentive Publications, Inc., 1969.

Croft, Doreen J., and Hess, Robert D. *An Activities Handbook for Teachers of Young Children.* Boston: Houghton Mifflin, 1975.

Daumer, Mary T. *Seasonal Kindergarten Units.* Belmont, Calif.: Fearon, 1972.

Ellis, Mary J. *Fingerplay Approach to Dramatization.* Minneapolis: Dennison, 1960.

Fleming, Bonnie Mack, and Hamilton, Darlene Softley. *Resources for Creative Teaching of Early Childhood Education.* New York: Harcourt Brace Jovanovich, 1977.

Forte, Imogene; Tangle, Mary Ann; and Rupa, Robbie. *Pumpkins, Pinwheels, and Peppermint Packages.* Nashville, Tenn.: Incentive Publications, Inc., 1974.

Fox, Helen. *Let's Go Places.* Minneapolis: Dennison, 1970.

Freedman, Miriam, and Perl, Teri. *A Sourcebook for Substitutes . . . and Other Teachers.* Reading, Mass.: Addison-Wesley, 1974.

Horn, George F. *Experiencing Art in the Kindergarten.* Worchester, Mass.: Davis, 1971.

Jorde, Paula. *The Kids Do It Book: A Handbook of Activities for Children From Three to Six.* San Francisco: New Glide, 1976.

Lorton, Mary Baratta. *Workjobs: Activity Centered Learning for Early Childhood Education.* Reading, Mass.: Addison-Wesley, 1972.

Malehorn, Hal. *Encyclopedia of Activities for Teaching Grades K-3.* West Nyack, N.Y.: Parker, 1975.

Mayesky, Mary, et al. *Creative Activities for Young Children.* Albany, New York: Delmar, 1975.

Miller, Mabel Evelyn. *Kindergarten Teacher's Activities Desk Book.* Englewood Cliffs, N.J.: Prentice-Hall, 1974.

Montgomery, Maxine. *Kindergarten Through the Years.* Minneapolis: Dennison, 1974.

Moore, Joan C. *Handbook for Kindergarten.* New York: Macmillan, 1967.
Myers, Gary C. *Headwork for Preschoolers.* Columbus, Ohio: Highlights Handbooks, 1968.
Newbury, Josephine. *More Kindergarten Resources.* Atlanta: John Knox Press, 1974.
Schaefer, Charles E. *Becoming Somebody: Creative Experiences for Preschool Children.* Buffalo, N.J.: DOK, 1973.
Vogels, Mary P. *Action Plays for Little Hands.* Minneapolis: Dennison, 1971.
Young, Ethel. *Amazing Life Games Theater.* Boston: Houghton Mifflin, 1971.

The following references are suggested for additional information concerning the education of children at the pre-first grade level:

Adams, Anne H. *A Book for Parents and Other Important People.* San Rafael, Calif.: Leswing Press, 1977.
Adams, Anne H., et al. *Threshold Learning Activities: Diagnostic and Instructional Activities for Specific Early Learning Disabilities.* New York: Macmillan, 1972.
Anderson, Verna Dieckman. *Reading and Young Children.* New York: Macmillan, 1968.
Dawson, Mildred A., and Newman, Georgiana Collis. *Language Teaching in Kindergarten and the Early Primary Grades.* New York: Harcourt, Brace & World, 1966.
Durkin, Dolores. *Teaching Them to Read.* Boston: Allyn and Bacon, 1974.
Flavell, John. *The Development of Role-taking and Communication Skills in Children.* New York: John Wiley & Sons, 1968.
Frost, Joe L., and Kissinger, Joan B. *The Young Child and the Educative Process.* New York: Holt, Rinehart and Winston, 1976.
Hildebrand, Verna. *Guiding Young Children.* New York: Macmillan, 1975.
Hipple, Marjorie L. *Early Childhood Education: Problems and Methods.* Santa Monica, Calif.: Goodyear, 1975.
Leeper, Sarah Hammond, et al. *Good Schools for Young Children.* New York: Macmillan, 1974.
Margolin, Edythe. *Young Children: Their Curriculum and Learning Processes.* New York: Macmillan, 1976.
Meyers, Elizabeth S., et al. *The Kindergarten Teacher's Handbook.* Los Angeles: Gramercy Press, 1973.
Moffett, James, and Wagner, Betty Jane. *Student-Centered Language Arts and Reading, K–13.* Boston: Houghton Mifflin, 1976.
Rudolph, Marguerita, and Cohen, Dorothy H. *Kindergarten: A Year of Learning.* New York: Appleton-Century-Crofts, 1964.
Ward, Muriel. *Young Minds Need Something to Grow On.* New York: Row, Peterson and Company, 1957.
Widmer, Emmy Louise. *Early Childhood Education at the Crossroads.* Scranton: International Textbook Co., 1970.
Wills, Clarice Dechent, and Lindberg, Lucile. *Kindergarten for Today's Children.* Chicago: Follett, 1967.

appendix one
The Lessons

LESSON	PICTURE/WORD ASSOCIATION MODULE	ALPHABET MODULE	ORAL LANGUAGE/ READING MODULE	STORY TIME MODULE
1	PHASE I WORDS (See Chapter Two, especially Steps 1-11, on how to teach this module) face	PHASE I LOWER CASE LETTERS (See Chapter Three on how to teach this module) l Art: draw a ladder	PHASE I SINGLE WORDS SPOKEN BY STUDENTS (See Chapter Four on how to teach this module) Discussion: toys	PHASE I WORDS WRITTEN BEFORE THE STORY IS READ (See Chapter Five on how to teach this module) characters in the story
2	animals	t Art: Draw a tree	Discussion: toys	names of places in the story
3	buildings	f Art: Draw a fan	Discussion: food	verbs in the story
4	fall	h Art: Draw a house	Discussion: food	names
5	school	**d** Students find words containing **d** in newspapers	Discussion: television	adjectives

LESSON	PICTURE/WORD ASSOCIATION MODULE	ALPHABET MODULE	ORAL LANGUAGE/ READING MODULE	STORY TIME MODULE
6	furniture	**i** Art: Draw a pig. (The letter **i** does not have to be in the initial position)	Discussion: television	words denoting different times
7	feet	**j** Art: Draw a jar	Discussion: pretty things	words for things that happened in the story
8	adults	**a** Art: Draw an apple	Discussion: pretty things	names
9	food	**p** Art: Draw a cap	Discussion: school	something that caused something to happen
10	automobile	**b** Students use newspapers to locate words containing **b**	Discussion: school	a description of something
11	firefighters	**v** Art: Draw a vase	Discussion: animals	character names
12	physicians and nurses	**x** Art: Draw an ax	Discussion: animals	colors
13	mail carriers	**w** Art: Draw a wagon	Discussion: friends	important events
14	police officers	**y** Art: Draw a yo-yo	Discussion: friends	sight words
15	teachers	**u** Students use newspapers to locate words containing **u**	Discussion: shopping	names of places
16	dentists	**z** Art: Draw a zipper	Discussion: shopping	objects
17	safety	**m** Art: Draw a man	Discussion: older people	movable items
18	trees	**n** Art: Draw a can	Discussion: older people	emotions

LESSON	PICTURE/WORD ASSOCIATION MODULE	ALPHABET MODULE	ORAL LANGUAGE/ READING MODULE	STORY TIME MODULE
19	street intersections or a road	r Art: Draw a rabbit	Discussion: playing	things that are seen
20	vegetables	c Students use newspapers to locate words containing **c**	Discussion: playing	things that are felt
21	Beginning with Lesson 21, when students have had opportunities to volunteer words for the chart, develop one sentence using some of the words on the chart. Write the sentence at the bottom of the chart. See Step 11, Chapter Two. moon	e Art: Draw an egg	Discussion: younger people	things that have odors
22	table tops	o Art: Draw a doll	Discussion: younger people	things that are heard
23	teeth	k Art: Draw a kite	Discussion: any two items	character names
24	flag	g Art: Draw a girl	Discussion: any two items	words denoting different sizes
25	school bus	s Students use newspapers to locate words containing s	Discussion: happiness	sight words
26	sky	q Art: Draw a queen's crown	Discussion: happiness	funny words
27	fingers	**PHASE II UPPER CASE LETTERS** **L**	Discussion: love	colors
28	horses	**T**	Discussion: love	adjectives in the story
29	rain	**F**	Discussion: desserts	verbs in the story

LESSON	PICTURE/WORD ASSOCIATION MODULE	ALPHABET MODULE	ORAL LANGUAGE/ READING MODULE	STORY TIME MODULE
30	machinery	**A** Students use news-papers to locate words containing **A**	Discussion: desserts	names of places
31	snakes	**H**	Discussion: sadness	character ages
32	airplanes	**J**	Discussion: sadness	objects that can be seen
33	cows	**K**	Discussion: working	character names
34	chairs	**P**	Discussion: working	words denoting time
35	stores	**B** Students use news-papers to locate words containing **B**	Discussion: energy	sight words
36	parents	**V**	Discussion: energy	emotions
37	clocks	**X**	Discussion: responsibility	descriptions
38	bicycles	**W**	Discussion: responsibility	items in the story
39	dogs	**Y**	Discussion: scary things	verbs
40	snow	**U** Students use news-papers to locate words containing **U**	Discussion: scary things	common noun
41	**PHASE II SINGLE WORDS AND WORD CLUSTERS** Begining with Lesson 41, have at least one word cluster on each chart and encourage students to give more than one word for items selected in the picture. plants	**Z**	Discussion: funny things	things that are heard

LESSON	PICTURE/WORD ASSOCIATION MODULE	ALPHABET MODULE	ORAL LANGUAGE/ READING MODULE	STORY TIME MODULE
42	athletes	**M**	Discussion: funny things	character names
43	desks	**N**	Discussion: feelings	verbs
44	walls	**R**	Discussion: feelings	nouns
45	stairs	**C** Students use newspapers to locate words containing **C**	Discussion: growing up	sight words
46	eyes	**E**	Discussion: growing up	adjectives
47	beach	**O**	Discussion: green things	names of places in the story
48	mountains	**D**	Discussion: green things	words denoting size
49	games	**G**	Discussion: any three items	feelings mentioned or inferred in the story
50	streets	**S** Students use newspapers to locate words containing **S**	Discussion: any three items	words ending in *ed*
51	houses	**I**	Discussion: noisy things	words ending in *ing*
52	boats	**Q**	Discussion: noisy things	sight words
53	woods	**PHASE III INITIAL PATTERNING** gr	Discussion: smooth things	colors
54	clothes	**sp**	Discussion: smooth things	character names
55	water	**fr** Students use newspapers to locate words containing **f**, **r**, or **fr**	Discussion: silence	adjectives

LESSON	PICTURE/WORD ASSOCIATION MODULE	ALPHABET MODULE	ORAL LANGUAGE/ READING MODULE	STORY TIME MODULE
56	trees	bl	Discussion: silence	nouns
57	trucks	br	Discussion: gentleness	words with suffixes
58	fire	fl	Discussion: gentleness	silly parts in the story
59	paper products	pl	Discussion: tiny things	words with prefixes
60	ears	sl Students use news-papers to locate words containing s, l, or sl	Discussion: tiny things	words for emotions in the story
61	people	sh	Discussion: things that move	objects in the story
62	scientist	sm	Discussion: things that move	sight words
63	meats	tr	Discussion: rules	prepositional phrases
64	neighbors	wh	Discussion: rules	places
65	containers	th Students use news-papers to locate words containing t, h, or th	Discussion: hot things	descriptions of characters
66	fruit	cl	Discussion: hot things	funny words
67	tools	sk	Discussion: blue things	descriptions of places
68	lights	st	Discussion: blue things	description of objects
69	floors	sw	Discussion: giant things	sight words

LESSON	PICTURE/WORD ASSOCIATION MODULE	ALPHABET MODULE	ORAL LANGUAGE/ READING MODULE	STORY TIME MODULE
70	boxes	**spl** Students use newspapers to locate words containing s, p, l, or **spl**	Discussion: giant things	verbs
71	stars	**spr**	Discussion: places	numbers
72	cities	**thr**	Discussion: places	words for things that move
73	fish	**PHASE IV RHYMING** red	Discussion: time	adjectives
74	bridges	**drill**	Discussion: time	verbs
75	boats	**cup**	Discussion: things that hurt	colors
76	astronauts	**frog**	Discussion: things that hurt	descriptions
77	fog	**charm**	Discussion: exciting things	words describing time
78	crowds	**pain**	Discussion: exciting things	words about the environment in the story
79	desert	**grind**	Discussion: success	character names
80	tracks	**blame**	Discussion: success	words denoting emotions
81	parts of the body	**car**	**PHASE II PICTURE/ WORD ASSOCIATIONS** Discussion: a person	**PHASE II CLUSTERWORDS WRITTEN BEFORE OR AFTER THE STORY IS READ** important words
82	food categories	**nail**	Discussion: a place	characters

LESSON	PICTURE/WORD ASSOCIATION MODULE	ALPHABET MODULE	ORAL LANGUAGE/ READING MODULE	STORY TIME MODULE
83	birds	**map**	Discussion: an item on a table	places
84	winter	**rake**	Discussion: a big thing	transportation in the story
85	tape recorders	**close**	Discussion: a little thing	references to food
86	squares	**leaf**	Discussion: two people	words in the story denoting size
87	children	**dime**	Discussion: two places	words in the story denoting places
88	houses	**brain**	Discussion: two items on a table	sight words
89	summer	**table**	Discussion: two big things	emotions indicated in the story
90	rectangles	**same**	Discussion: two little things	adjectives used in the story
91	spring	**fog**	Discussion: airplanes	objects named in the story
92	sounds	**light**	Discussion: automobiles	verbs used in the story
93	outdoor animals	**growl**	Discussion: music	character names
94	indoor animals	**slow**	Discussion: trucks	sight words
95	circles	**wall**	Discussion: a rainy day	nice things in the story
96	clocks	**Jack**	Discussion: inside a refrigerator	prepositional phrases
97	tastes	**Nell**	Discussion: the dentist	pretty items in the story
98	musical instruments	**Spring**	Discussion: a safe thing to do	objects in the story
99	sandwiches	**cow**	Discussion: birthday	places

LESSON	PICTURE/WORD ASSOCIATION MODULE	ALPHABET MODULE	ORAL LANGUAGE/ READING MODULE	STORY TIME MODULE
100	insects	sit	Discussion: a holiday	events in the story
101	television stars	**PHASE V VARIOUS SOUNDS OF VOWELS** ee (flee)	**PHASE III SENTENCES CONTAINING A SPECIFIC WORD CLUSTER THEME** jumping in the air	**PHASE II WORDS WRITTEN BEFORE OR AFTER THE STORY IS READ** rhyming words
102	turtles	**a_e (cake)**	jumping in the air	emotions
103	yo-yos	**i_e (mice)**	getting shoes	words ending in *ed*
104	hills	**o (go)**	getting shoes	adjectives
105	kings and queens	**u_e (glue)**	bouncing a ball	colors
106	rabbits	**o_e (nose)**	bouncing a ball	sight words
107	frisbees	**igh (fight)**	brushing my teeth	exciting words
108	circus	**y (shy)**	brushing my teeth	names of animals
109	witches	**oa (boat)**	licking a lollipop	verbs
110	lions, tigers, ape, etc.	**ow (slow)**	licking a lollipop	nouns
111	books	**a (rat)**	combing my hair	prepositional phrases
112	zoo	**u (bug)**	combing my hair	character names
113	cartoon characters	**i (big)**	dancing to music	things in the story that are heard
114	parrot	**e (bed)**	dancing to music	silly parts in the story

LESSON	PICTURE/WORD ASSOCIATION MODULE	ALPHABET MODULE	ORAL LANGUAGE/ READING MODULE	STORY TIME MODULE
115	puzzles	**oo** **(look)**	visiting a friend	places
116	bus station, airport, etc.	**ow** **(cow)**	visiting a friend	contractions
117	bubble gum	**or** **(stork)**	riding in a car	adjectives describing people
118	library	**oo** **(soon)**	riding in a car	sight words
119	rainbows	**ur** **(fur)**	tying my shoelaces	exciting parts in the story
120	oceans	**aw** **(law)**	tying my shoelaces	something sad
121	hamburgers	**PHASE VI LABELING OBJECTS IN THE CLASSROOM** **chalkboard (ch)** **light (l)**	reading a book	words ending in *ing*
122	jelly beans	**desk (d)** **window (w)**	reading a book	adjectives
123	hot dogs	**book (b)** **floor (fl)**	eating candy	numbers
124	windows	**pencil (p)** **corner (c)**	eating candy	things that are heard
125	different kinds of clothing	**girl (g)** **yardstick (y)**	talking with my teacher	words denoting time
126	**PHASE III SINGLE WORDS, WORD CLUSTERS, AND SENTENCES** Beginning with Lesson 126, develop at least one sentence in addition to the sentence at the bottom of the chart. Other items on the chart can be single words or word clusters. rocks	**hand (h)** **milk (m)** **vase (v)**	talking with my teacher	exciting words

LESSON	PICTURE/WORD ASSOCIATION MODULE	ALPHABET MODULE	ORAL LANGUAGE/ READING MODULE	STORY TIME MODULE
127	roads	**nursery rhymes** (r) **newspapers** (n)	playing with friends	adjectives describing places
128	ants	**student** (st) **van** (v)	playing with friends	words ending in *ed*
129	pigs	**teacher** (t) **foot** (f)	painting a picture	movable items
130	bears	**jar** (j) **key** (k)	painting a picture	important events
131	drug stores	**PHASE VII ALPHABET LETTER DICTATION** **l**	looking at the moon	words for emotions in the story
132	grocery stores	**g**	looking at the moon	places
133	baseball field	**wh**	watching a television program	number of characters in the story
134	ice cream	**sp**	watching a television program	sentences in the story
135	strawberries	**m**	sitting in a chair	verbs
136	carrots	**str**	sitting in a chair	words ending in *ing*
137	appliances	**ch**	building a block castle	sight words
138	keys	**f**	building a block castle	words denoting time
139	basketball players	**r**	stringing colored beads	sequence of events
140	gerbils	**k** or **c**	stringing colored beads	modes of transportation
141	sandboxes	**s**	taking a trip	colors in the story
142	balls	**d**	taking a trip	character names
143	tents	**t**	eating an ice cream cone	emotions

LESSON	PICTURE/WORD ASSOCIATION MODULE	ALPHABET MODULE	ORAL LANGUAGE/ READING MODULE	STORY TIME MODULE
144	toys	p	eating an ice cream cone	unhappy characters
145	sticks	b	playing hide and seek	exciting parts of the story
146	princes	h	playing hide and seek	funny words
147	exercise	m	jumping with a rope	happy parts in the story
148	football players	w	jumping with a rope	colors
149	presidents	th	getting ready for school	verbs
150	packages	j	getting ready for school	important parts in the story
151	country scene	st	eating lunch	something pretty
152	liquids	n	eating lunch	nicest persons in the story
153	waves	fl	blowing up a balloon	happiest characters
154	city scene	qu	blowing up a balloon	adjectives
155	bandages	**PHASE VIII CONSONANT COMPLETION** -ake	helping at home	exciting parts in the story
156	medicine	-ine	helping at home	sight words
157	frogs	-eek	listening to a story	objects
158	radios	-ate	listening to a story	emotions
159	fish	-een	taking a ride	words for places in the story
160	mice	-at	taking a ride	items in the story
161	hats	-ow	watching a storm	main characters

LESSON	PICTURE/WORD ASSOCIATION MODULE	ALPHABET MODULE	ORAL LANGUAGE/ READING MODULE	STORY TIME MODULE
162	tractors	**-oon**	watching a storm	places
163	fences	**-oke**	watching a game	prepositional phrases
164	cereals	**-one**	watching a game	words ending with plural *s*
165	peanut butter	**-ale**	getting my hair cut	words ending with *ing*
166	parties	**-ile**	getting my hair cut	silly words
167	apples	**-ool**	eating a snack	things that are seen
168	grandparents	**-ean**	eating a snack	verbs
169	clowns	**-ute**	finding a secret place	final events
170	bananas	**-eel**	finding a secret place	sight words
171	breads	**-um**	getting presents	occupations in the story
172	potatoes	**-ing**	getting presents	funny words
173	trains	**-ed**	waving goodbye	words for feelings in the story
174	the sun	**-ir**	waving goodbye	sad words
175	clouds	**-oy**	jumping over a puddle	nouns
176	buckets	**-ore**	jumping over a puddle	nice feelings in the story
177	signs	**-ule**	thinking by myself	adjectives
178	principals	**-ail**	thinking by myself	words related to time
179	teachers	**-ack**	talking on the tele-phone	verbs
180	friends	**-ight**	talking on the tele-phone	exciting words in the story

appendix two
Checklist for Teachers, Other Educators, and Visitors

The following is a list of some of the important components in the *Success in Kindergarten Reading and Writing* program. Refer to the appropriate chapter for additional information concerning any item in the list.

GENERAL

___ 1. Schedule three 20 minute modular instructional times—(1) Picture/Word Association Module, (2) Alphabet Module, and (3) Story Time Module.

___ 2. Schedule one individual module with as many students as possible each day—Oral Language/Reading Module.

___ 3. Use a variety of materials including fiction and nonfiction books, newspapers, magazines, catalogues, boxes, labels, telephone books, comics, encyclopedias, etc.

___ 4. Use the newspaper and discuss at least one part of it and some current events with the class each day.

___ 5. Introduce students to reading and writing in a natural, rather than artificial manner.

___ 6. Work individually with every child in each module each day.

___ 7. Do not divide students into "ability" groups.

___ 8. Do not expect mastery; instead, help each student achieve some degree of success in each module.

PICTURE/WORD ASSOCIATION MODULE

___ 1. Write student-volunteered words beside a picture on chart paper each day. Individual students volunteer words.

___ 2. Draw a line from each word to the item in the picture.

___ 3. Say each letter as you write it. Encourage members of the class to say the letters with you.

___ 4. Help the class create a title for each picture.

___ 5. Help the class write a sentence containing some of the words on the chart.

___ 6. Display the chart in the classroom.

___ 7. Include words for tangible items and intangible concepts in the discussions.

___ 8. Use a wide variety of pictures during the academic year. Change the picture topic and discussion emphasis each day.

ALPHABET MODULE

___ 1. Change the writing symbol(s) daily.

___ 2. Correlate student artwork with letter formation.

___ 3. During the writing, move around the classroom giving assistance to individual students.

___ 4. As the students' abilities increase, expand the art/writing correlation to include words, word clusters, and sentences.

___ 5. Incorporate the use of newspapers in the Alphabet Module.

___ 6. Each student dates and files his or her paper developed each day during this module in a folder.

___ 7. Send the folder containing student work from the Alphabet Module home at the end of the year.

___ 8. Send papers from other parts of the school day home frequently.

ORAL LANGUAGE/READING MODULE

___ 1. Work with students on a one-to-one basis at any convenient time during the school day.

___ 2. Record on separate strips of paper at least one word spoken by each student during the Oral Language/Reading Module.

___ 3. Use puppets and/or pictures in some conversations.

___ 4. Each student displays in the classroom the paper strip containing his or her words.

___ 5. Develop themes within each discussion. Change the theme or discussion focus daily.

STORY TIME MODULE

___ 1. Write on the chalkboard a few categorical words or word clusters.

___ 2. Read fiction to the class each day during the Story Time Module.

___ 3. At least once, refer to the words on the chalkboard during the reading of the story.

___ 4. Refer to the words during a review/discussion of parts of the story after the story is finished.

___ 5. Provide different library books in the classroom on a variety of reading levels throughout the year.

Index